Emoji

50 Easy Ways to Overcome Anxiety and Find Your Happy Face

The Go-to Wellness Guide for All Ages

SHARON CHEMELLO

TLC: Tough Love Coaching: Heart Centred Coaching for Families

EMOJI- 50 Easy Ways to Overcome Anxiety and Find Your Happy Face
The Go-to Wellness Guide for All Ages

By Sharon Chemello
Foreword by Paul Williams
First Edition 2022
Copyright c. 2022 *Tough Love Coaching: Heart Centred Coaching for Families*
All rights reserved. No part of this publication may be reproduced, stored in a retrieval system, or transmitted in any form or by any means, electronic, mechanical, photocopying, recording or otherwise, without the prior written permission from both the copyright owner and publisher.

Disclaimer
All the information, techniques, skills, and concepts contained within this publication are of the nature of general comment and are not in any way recommended as individual advice. The intent is to offer a variety of information to provide a wider range of choices now and in the future, recognising that we all have widely diverse circumstances and viewpoints. Should any reader choose to make use of the information contained herein, this is their decision and the author and publishers do not assume any responsibilities whatsoever under condition or circumstances.
ISBN: 978-0-6455959-0-1 (Paperback)

For more information about the author, Sharon Chemello, or for additional trainings, speaking engagements, or media enquiries, please visit Sharon Chemello, Facebook. https://www.facebook.com/sharon.chemello (See also contact details in back of book.)

Connect with Sharon Chemello:

Email: s.e.chemello27@gmail.com
LinkedIn: Sharon Chemello
Instagram: Sharon_Chemello_Emoji
Facebook: Sharon Chemello
Tough Love Coaching: Heart Centred Coaching for Families.
Sustainable Crusaders. (With Frank)
Sleep Better without Drugs. (With Dr David Morawetz.)
Groups: EMOJI: Find your Happy face! Shared strategies for wellness and joy! The Confidence Academy. The Kid, Teen and Families Whisperers, support during challenging times.
Cover photo: Saint Stephen›s Green Park, Dublin, Ireland. May 2020 by Jacqueline Munguia
Cover Design & Format: Ash, Change Maker Press

*Dance like no one's watching,
sing like no one's listening,
love like you've never been hurt
and live each day as if it were your last.
And don't wait for the storm to pass,
dance in the rain!
To Marco, Lisa, Frank and Mum.*

Foreword

I first met Sharon and began working with her in 2021. When Sharon asked me if I would write the foreword to her book, my initial reaction was one of delight. Books have always been a very important part of my life. It is an honour to be a part of something which will truly help others better their understanding of trauma and learn ways to turn their pain into healing.

I've really enjoyed sitting down in my chair at home with a hot drink and reading "EMOJI". I admire that Sharon has created this book with new readers in mind, as I believe there are so many out there just embarking on their journey of healing.

This book is not only informative, but also extremely practical. EMOJI offers people many options to find the healing they seek. I love strategies and solutions. That is why I have read the number of books I have.

Over the past 12 years, I have read more than 200 books. I have, predominantly, been drawn to self-help and spiritual books as a resource and inspiration for my own healing journey.

When I was young, I was diagnosed with dyslexia. This condition is defined as a learning disorder that involves difficulty reading due to problems identifying speech sounds and learning how they relate to letters and words. When I received my diagnosis as a child, the condition was not well understood. What I did understand was that I was different in a myriad of ways from those around me.

I learned slowly to read by learning in a unique way that I was able to understand. It has served as a great testament to overcoming adversity. Often, we find ourselves in situations in life that are unfavourable. Learning to create the reality that we desire by never giving up, remaining consistent and persistent has been one of my life's greatest lessons.

EMOJI contains many powerful ideas, one that resonated with me in particular, is the inclusion of the quote from his holiness The Dalai Lama, "Pain is inevitable, suffering is a choice." Boy, that is such a fitting statement for my own life! I have learned that suffering is indeed a choice. That kind emoji happy face that we all know, in the midst of pain and suffering, is perhaps the beginning.

What the pandemic gifted us was the chance to slow down, go within, better understand ourselves and, I hope, others also.

As Sharon so finely articulates in the opening of this book, the information readers will discover has come from her one-on-one work with individuals during her time as a coach.

I have experienced depression and anxiety over the years due to what Sharon describes as "chemicals". However, as she so acutely writes, "WE make the chemicals."

The late great Dolores Cannon said, "You are the producer, director, and actor in your own play, you're also the scriptwriter. The script is being written as it goes along. You can change the script anytime you want". To say that this is not only a profound statement but also a self-empowering one would be an understatement.

Sharon writes much on anxiety and depression to help people understand more about them while also offering tools to help people change their life - or their script.

What I love about EMOJI, is Sharon's way of integrating spiritual teachings - the Dalai Lama, Wim Hof to name a few- with the scientific work of the late David Hawkins. My own work encompasses the blend of spirituality and science and I have found the two complement each other quite beautifully.

I trust you will resonate with Sharon's bravery, authenticity, vulnerability, and compassion- as I have in reading this book.

Paul Williams
QHHT* Practitioner, Delores Cannon Method, Transformational Speaker and Coach.

September 12th, 2022

Dedication

To Marco and Lisa, (and Crystal and Dylan) my amazing millennials, to Frank my wonderful, supportive partner and my smart, strong, and patient Mum.

To little Sharon, and big kid Sharon, who always had the wisdom, thanks for being you! Thanks for hanging in there so I could catch up with you.

Karen and Simone, my best supporters, and friends. To all my coaches and friends in the coaching world. To all my mates and family. To everyone who has supported my journey and EMOJI model.

And Basil the Brilliant Dog, for always being here.

For Heather, who left us last year, an amazing coach and special friend. For your inspiration and for being awesomely *flawesome*.

☺ The Go-to Wellness Guide for All Ages ☺

Table of Contents

Foreword V
Dedication ix
Preface 01

☺ Chapter 1: Introduction. 05
☺ Chapter 2: How to use this book 19
☺ Chapter 3: EMOJI 35
☺ Chapter 4: Anxiety and Depression 41
☺ Chapter 5: Modalities, Strategies, Ideas. 49
☺ Chapter 6: E 59
☺ Chapter 7: M 83
☺ Chapter 8: O 111
☺ Chapter 9: J 133
☺ Chapter 10: I 145
☺ Chapter 11: What's Next? 175
☺ Chapter 12: Closing Words and Thank-Yous. .. 181

Testimonials 191
Appendix 197
Resources And References 202
Emoji Index 211
About The Author 215

Preface

"You may never have proof of your importance, but you are more important than you think. There are always those who couldn't do without you. The rub is that you don't always know who."

— *Robert Fulghum, All I Really Need to Know I Learned in Kindergarten*

"What's coming up for us is to leave us." Andrew Pearce, Australian Coach.

"Pain is inevitable, suffering is a choice." Dalai Lama.

There are some sections repeated in this book as I want it to be a "dip in" book where you can use the Index to help you find what you want quickly.

EMOJI: Find your happy face! (Thanks to Frank for this title.)

To the kids in Petrie, north of Brisbane, at the high school, many of whom are kids with *additional needs*, who danced in the rain with me when I told them the ways I have learned to deal with anxiety and shared Emoji with them. When a student said to me "You wouldn't understand Miss, I have anxiety."

I thought "Wow, where do I start?" I drew a deep breath. I paused. They listened.

I wrote EMOJI on the whiteboard.

I told them my story in brief, a few minutes, about a good and generally happy life, but a life also full of anxiety and challenges. (These kids were around sixteen, seventeen years of age.) I kept it light, not too much detail or scary stuff. Boy, did they listen! Adults maybe don't share enough with kids. When you share with vulnerability, people listen.

> "When you share with vulnerability, honesty, and real experience, you help to normalise mental health. This is vital. Discussing mental health should be as "normal" as discussing asthma. Only then can we begin to help heal the collective. Only then can we reduce the self-harm and suicide rates." ***Sharon Chemello.***

I outlined a few strategies that have worked for me. A few looked on with doubt or suspicion. So, I showed them!

I said, "Everyone come outside, take off your shoes." Some did, some didn't. That's ok. I started dancing near a tree around a large rock. Some joined in with passion, dancing and laughing, some watched, mostly laughing. Some stood back, reserved, yet started laughing and enjoying the show. It started to rain lightly. Some wanted to go back in. I said "Sure, or we could dance in the rain."

So, we did. Well, some of us.

When we went back inside the classroom, there was a lot of laughter and real joy. I talked about the chemicals we had released. I asked them how they now felt. I did explain this is just a simple quick fix and that dealing with anxiety and depression can take much more and to ask your parents if you can see a professional, if you feel you need to. You can get free mental health care through your doctor. I told them about many groups such as *Headspace, Kids' Help Line, Beyond Blue, Reach Out and Black Dog.* School counsellors, teachers. That you can always, always reach out! That no one should ever feel alone.

I told Emma, my publishing coach, the story this morning on my final day of writing, and we agreed to put it at the start of the book. It's in the thankyous, in brief, at the end of the book, however this story deserves more. It demonstrates the power of Emoji. A bunch of shared wellness strategies (ideas) that help our wellness, creating joy, peace, and calm.

My good friend and coach Michelle suggested that "*strategies*" sounds a bit too clinical and scientific, maybe "*ideas*" is more creative and fun. Thanks Michelle. I will use both.

Whenever you see something in this book in italics, it's really important. Maybe go buy a journal or scrapbook to write them down or pop them on a notice board for the whole family, or just yourself for your journey.

*Whenever you see an asterisk and italics, it's an idea TO TRY! Please do try it and even let me know in the EMOJI group (details in the back of this book) how you go, I genuinely want to know! It thrills me when people tell me a strategy or idea that I have suggested has worked for them. If you prefer to keep it to yourself, that's ok too. There are no rules here! Choose your own adventure!

Chapter 1.
Introduction.

Many of the strategies (ideas) in Emoji, you already know. Sometimes we just don't do them. We play games on computers or phones, watch TV, You Tube, or Netflix, scroll through social media, eat takeaway and sugar, sometimes drink caffeine and alcohol and wonder why we are anxious and not as happy as others. We hang onto "past baggage" and relationship dramas, we react rather than respond to life and we worry. With EMOJI, you can break free of all of this. So can your family/ friends/ partners if you teach them or share this with them. You might even try your very first meditation ever! Some of the strategies will be new for you to try if you wish. Start by going outside and moving! Notice the difference.

I messaged Paul Williams, a top-level Australian coach with a huge following, to ask him if he would write the foreword for this book. He said Yes! Paul is an amazing young man with so much wisdom, and he was once sad. He was bullied. He was overweight. Now he is fit and happy. He teaches meditation and he has trained in the Delores Cannon method of Quantum Healing Hypnosis Technique. He is a coach, speaker, and author. We became friends when someone in a group for mental health, challenged me to ask him for an interview. He said yes to that too. But what's important here is, I accepted the challenge and asked.

Here's the first thing to learn, because it's important to know when you are reading this book. Pop this on a sticky note on your bathroom mirror. Better still, set up a notice board, or household or family notice board with these kinds of notes, quotes, and models for personal development. You will need this one the most to try new things.

Stepping outside your comfort zone is where the learning and growth occur.

(Various people.)

Here's what I think this book is about, in a nutshell.

Personal development, or self-help and wellness strategies (ideas) for *newbies*. (I had thought of using the word *dummies* like the computer books for dummies that used to be a thing, but you're no dummy! You just don't know what you don't know and might need a little help to find the answers.)

More ideas for Personal Development junkies (followers) like me.

Dealing with/ reducing/overcoming/ facing and accepting anxiety and depression. *More about this later.*

Ways to find more peace, calm and joy.

Ways to let go of what doesn't "*serve us.*" Otherwise known as *unresourceful behaviours*.

A book to help you, or someone you care about.

*Learn more *resourceful behaviours*. There are so many here in this book!

Some call strategies like this a "tool kit". My coach, Emma, referred to a "*well*" of ideas and knowledge. I like that analogy. For my coaching, I bought a Mary Poppins carpet (tapestry) bag. If you have ever watched Mary Poppins, the bag is bottomless, infinite. A bit like a well. I've even called it my tool kit. Teenagers love it. *"What's in the bag?"* In the bag, I keep books, cards, crystals, oils, charts, props; things that might support our work when I visit clients face to face. I also use it in my Facetime or Zoom calls with clients.

This book is a summary of about six or seven years of personal development, or self-help, and coaching. I hope it helps you or someone you love or care about. I want it to be suitable for the whole family. At least for parents to share ideas with kids. For anyone who is overwhelmed, stressed, anxious, depressed, addicted to something, struggling in relationships, family breakdown, or just wanting more happiness in their life. Or for someone in your life, please gift this book. It might be the best gift you ever give someone. I hope so. I hope I can shortcut the system for you. Help you to find answers more quickly and less expensively than I did.

More shortly on who this book is for and how to use it.

EMOJI came to me in a blinding flash while I was on a walk doing a live video about strategies for wellness. And here it is, I hope it helps you find some ways to learn, feel, deal, and heal. It has helped me and many others I have helped.

About me.

My bio is in the back of this book. *About the Author*. You'll find out more about me as you work your way through this book. I have included many stories of my journey and finding my EMOJI that I hope will help you.

I have written a chapter for a book called *"55 Faces"* with Michelle Gardiner, a coaching friend who lives in Bali. I've written a chapter for "Change Makers Volume 6", published by Emma Hamlin (my publishing coach for this book).

Here is the *story* version of why I know I have enough knowledge, experience, and background to share with you some of what I have learned along the way. This version is more about my **why**.

This is the sort of kid I was and still am. Looking for something special. Looking for answers. Are you? If so, read on.

About seven years ago, I was on the couch crying, just separated, later divorced, anxious, depressed, drinking, eating whole tubs of ice cream or blocks of chocolate, staying up way too late, watching bad TV, dating badly, angry, hurt, ashamed, guilty. Messed up big time. My poor kids.

Thanks for your patience, guys. I'm back. Well actually, a new and better me. Now I can finally be the mum I want to be. They were seventeen and nineteen when I left home. What a terrible time to leave them. I'm so sorry, they know. I am forgiven. Lisa says we are all better off. Thanks Lisa. Marco just says "Meh." Love those kids!

Forgiving yourself is the hardest part. All part of the journey.

For younger readers, or if reading to younger family members, I had an anxious childhood and teen years. I messed up many things, especially in relationships. I felt the three universal fears, commonly recognised by coaches: *not being good enough or worthy, not being loved (perhaps in the way we felt we needed) and not belonging. Cited and adapted by many coaches including Gregg Braden. Also: fear of trusting and surrendering, (aligns with not being worthy or good enough) abandonment and separation (not belonging).*

This continued into my adult years as I didn't know what help I needed. I masked the pain and drank. When I had my own kids, I struggled. I was a good wife and mum on the outside, but inside I was a mess. I did a lot of bad stuff. I have made the best amends I can and am living a better life every day. *I am learning to look forward, not back.*

Before we go back in time, here's who I am today. I'm a teacher and life coach. I teach Prep to Year Twelve. I mostly coach families, help kids and teens, and their parents. I do coach adults as well. Some testimonials for my coaching are referenced at the back of this book. They provide the views of those I have worked with and people who know me well. *They are also case studies in brief.*

I'm a mum of two amazing millennials, Marco, twenty-six and Lisa, twenty- four, at the time of publishing this book. I love their partners, Crystal, and Dylan. I'm a partner to Frank. I found Frank on a dating site after about fifty bad dates. Well, maybe ten good and forty bad. That story is for another book. Frank is amazing; supportive and lets me be me (most of the time). I've been searching for that all my life. Maybe he loves me for who I am. I'm a step-mum and even a step-grandmother now. I'm a friend and a daughter.

I am a traveller, always looking for somewhere to go. Next year, we plan to do a lap of Australia with a caravan and tinnie (small fishing boat). We will travel as *Sustainable Crusaders*. We are teaching sustainability in lifestyle and life. More about that later. I'm an adventurer, always trying new things, skateboarding, surfing, sky diving, Latin dance and more. And much more to try.

I am creative, I teach the Arts, I sing and play guitar. I love camping, the beach, and the bush. I love travelling overseas and have done quite a lot for which I am very grateful. I have ventured into a lot of real estate and renovations. I love gardening and cooking. I love fitness, yoga, and meditation. This is starting to sound like a dating profile. That'll do.

I also worked in sales and marketing for educational publishers for a few years and have always been good at "selling" ideas to people. I thank my Uncle Richard for some training and mentoring there. I hope I can "sell" EMOJI to you as a way of moving out of anxiety and into happiness.

I had a tough upbringing. Not like Tony Robbins, but enough to cause some pain that needed healing. I didn't start my healing journey proper until I was over fifty years old. You can start your journey any time. Let's hope a lot earlier than I did.

My dad was in the air force, so we moved a lot. This was hard for us all. But it helped me to learn to make friends easily. Everyone in my family had their struggles. Dad was a drinker and it messed with him. It caused a lot of trouble. Or rather, he caused a lot of trouble, partly because of the alcohol. He had his strengths; he was creative and inclusive. Mum was creative, strong, resilient, and knowledgeable.

Mum turns eighty this year, just before I turn sixty. She comes from a generation of people who *"didn't talk about it"* so this book will be hard for her. It's a brave new world and I need to be part of it. *If I help one person...*

My siblings both had what we now refer to in schools, as *special needs, or additional needs*. They had their challenges and strengths. Kim was very sweet and caring. Steven had a good sense of humour. They both struggled at school. Mum helped them a lot. Mum tried to juggle all that (with no parents, they had already died and no siblings) and one smart kid who was always pushing boundaries. I wanted it all. When they said I couldn't have a birthday party, I sent out invitations myself at six. (That didn't work by the way.)

When I couldn't go on a trip at eleven because we couldn't afford it, I raised money myself doing jobs around the neighbourhood. Mum and Dad matched the money I made and topped it up. I learned to play guitar and wrote songs. I went on TV at eleven. I auditioned for a part in a well-known Australian movie and was shortlisted. I filled out forty entries, with Dad's help, at the circus to win a minibike and won. If you told me that I couldn't do something I would find a way. (That hasn't changed!) I wasn't good at netball, so I went over to the school every time I could to practice, so I could be the best goal shooter ever to get into the team as Goal Attack. I learned to kick a football with John, my first sweetheart. When we moved to Malaysia, I did the same thing.

Whatever I wasn't good at, I would find a skill to practise to be included.

When we came back to Brisbane, I was mostly a good student, I got into the basketball team, musicals and became sports house captain. Remember I wasn't that good at sport. Just determined. (And a good leader.) When I was younger, Mum won the mother's running race at the school carnival. Determined. She wasn't good at sport. Dad was. My siblings weren't. I have such empathy for kids when I am teaching, and teams are rarely chosen by the kids. And when they're in a team, they must support each other. Everyone is important. If someone isn't good at something, I think it's our job to help them become better.

Despite all this, I never felt good enough. Not in my childhood, my adulthood, or my marriage. (It was generally a good marriage, or so I thought anyway.) I became the ultimate people pleaser always trying to achieve some recognition, accolades, love. I would overdo things. A habit I've worked on with one of my coaches, Andrew. I would get involved in way too much. Looking for something and avoiding my own inner pain.

(A common strategy used by people who have experienced trauma or feel unworthy. Is this you?)

Now I generally know what to prioritise and how to achieve goals. I'm still slow and a time waster, sometimes procrastinating or avoiding, yet I am getting there. Slow and steady wins the race.

I have more books to write, more people to teach, so much more to learn. More places to go. More songs to sing, poems to write, paintings to paint, instruments to learn, dances to try, people to meet and speeches to make. Watch this space! On this my last day of writing, Frank just brought me in another song he's writing. Wow! We have started something.

I've done six or seven years of studying personal development, self-help, and coaching. I've spent a great deal of time and money. I've read books, listened to podcasts, attended courses; short and long, studied many strategies and modalities. I've been coached by many of the best in the business. Thank you all!

What are you doing for healing, learning, growth? You can start here! Go grab a journal. Something to write down ideas. Go do that now and buy a meaningful one this week! With a front cover quote or cool title. I pick out a new one with a great heading, every few months. My latest says "Be you tifle."

I've found many answers and l will find and teach many more!

Testimonials for EMOJI.

"It's a terrific model to quickly get back on track by using simple but effective tips." *Karen, friend, and follower.*

"Hey guys, I don't know if you know this, but Sharon Chemello, one of our fellow Academy members is running a fantastic Facebook group that is a beautiful safe space to explore our many emotions and so much more....

Highly recommended that you take the time to have a look. Love hearts and praying hands emojis. "

Steve, top- level Australian coach. Posted kindly in his coaching group, I am Enough Academy.

"Hey everyone, I'm Simone and I've been involved in so many life-coaching programs with Aunty Shazza. The EMOJI MODEL is an amazing tool that I use every day. I especially love energy, emotional management, exercise, oils, own your shizzle, working on awareness of jealousy, judgement and justification and the inner child and inner work. Such amazing strategies to use in everyday life. (Love heart emojis.) *Simone, client, and friend.*

Chapter 2
How to use this book.

What should you do with this book? What others say...

I asked members of my Facebook group: "If you were writing a book called EMOJI: Find your happy face! Shared strategies for wellness and joy! (Working title and title of the Facebook group) What do you think would be the most important message?"

The group is full of coaches, people into personal development and regular people looking for answers and support. They have all been helping along the way with developing the model.

Here are their answers:

- Kelly: Read everything in this book.
- Johnno: Be cool! I asked how and he posted a John Travolta Pulp Fiction type cool GIF.
- Jason: It's your book and your message (which is not like Jason at all, normally he would give a smart assed answer. Must have had his coffee!) (We talked about where I'd fit coffee into Emoji this morning.) Maybe I will challenge him, just wait a minute. OK, so I've just said: "This is a very sensible answer, have you been hacked?" Waiting...
- Sharon L says: Allow yourself just to BE you and take whatever resources you need, do not feel you need to read the book cover to cover,

choose practices that work for you. Is Sharon L living in my head or what?

- Donna-Lee says to Sharon L: I like this. I can use the bee emoji. (Bee emoji.)
- Johnno says to Sharon L: Exactly Bee cool, then the sunglasses emoji.

Hey you lot! Just talk amongst yourselves, right? Don't mind me! You know, the author!

This is exactly what I've enjoyed about creating EMOJI, that everyone has ownership and contribution. And now significance as they see their name in the book. We have just answered two of Tony Robbins' six core needs: contribution and significance (Google these, super interesting!) and one of Emoji: Ownership!

Later, Donna-Lee says: *"Always strive to be happy!!*
Goes without saying hey?
Seriously, I had a little think and the core to finding happiness is .. Living consciously in the present
Being grateful even in testing times
Self-love
Perspective and ownership.
I am so proud of you Sharon Chemello! I can't wait for your book to be on the shelves!" Donna-Lee is a Happiness Coach in Perth.

We had a big post about coffee where I asked them all: "How can I fit Coffee into Emoji?" Great answers, ranging from E for energy and essential, to I for initiate the day, and even a poem by Bruce. Thanks team. I was hoping to pop it into the Appendix, but I cannot for the life of me find it! Perhaps I will do a new one. (Done!) You can find it on our page if you type "coffee"into the search.

My little red bible I was given at about age eleven. A short story of love and light.

When I was writing this book and having discussions with Emma, we talked about how it would be good to have an index with places to go for things like anxiety, depression, joy. Suddenly I remembered my little red bible, given to me when I was in primary (elementary) school by one of the lovely ladies from the church who would come around and teach us about Jesus. I remember asking Mum to write my name in it because she had "grownup" writing.

Over the years, especially in my teens, I clung onto the messages in that bible as it too had an index, "*Where to find help when...*" What a lovely memory. I think the bible is in storage, so next time I'm at the storage shed I will go in search and have it ready for the Emoji launch.

I just sent this snippet to Mum; I hope she enjoys it!

That's going straight to EMOJI!

There is a wonderful, iconic Australian film from the 1990s, called "The Castle" where members of the family find or buy treasures and they say, "That's going straight to the pool room" (where they play pool, billiards, or snooker.) As I was writing the book and interacting with people in the Facebook group, someone would suggest a strategy or idea and I would say *"That's going straight to EMOJI."* It became my catch cry when anyone submitted a great idea for the model.

One thing I did when writing this book, was to pose questions in the EMOJI Facebook group to find answers to many of these strategies to gather collective wisdom.

So, dear reader, (I've always wanted to say that) you benefit from the wisdom of many coaches and people into personal development in my group. How good is that?

Don't be Pollyanna!

This is NOT about putting on a brave face, being Pollyanna (a Disney character who always saw the bright side) or faking it until you make it! I did that for way too long! There are many things I love about Pollyanna, however, her positivity, gratitude, and inclusivity.

John Demartini says: *"Be clear on what you would love and be grateful for all that you already have. Positive thinking alone will not change lives, but balanced thinking, which opens the heart to gratitude and love will. See both sides, ask how what you think challenges you, serves you. This will lower your stress and increase your vitality and enthusiasm for living."*

A real disclaimer: I am not a doctor, or psychologist. I am a life coach, teacher, and Mum. I have a great deal of life experience and many studies. Not nearly as extensive as some coaches. The strategies in this book have helped many, there are many studies to prove their value. But I can offer no real guarantee on their results. But I do know they may absolutely work. I have many testimonials and my own experience to prove this. Sometimes I even experiment and check my mood before and after using an idea from EMOJI.

*It's up to you to try things and see how they go! Take action starting now. For you, for your family, partner, friends, but mostly for you!

Strategies (ideas) for wellness.

This is about genuine proven strategies (ideas) that have helped many to feel better, happier, more peaceful and calmer. More joy! I have seen some coaches say that writing gratitudes will not heal you, or "beat anxiety and depression" and they are correct to a point. Gratitude and affirmations can't be forced. They just won't work.

If you have some big baggage you are hanging onto, you must find ways to heal that as part of your journey. If not for you, for your kids and those around you. But mostly for you to find peace. **Sharon Chemello.**

These are great starting points for your journey. Some coaches say we don't need fixing. We are not broken. Whilst I agree to a point and that's a great sentiment, some people have no idea where to start to heal.

Some coaches say "*The answers are within you*" yet some of us have no idea how to find them.

Even as I write this, I am working with a coach, digging deeper on some issues I am still having trouble with "letting go." A coach I have worked with many times over the past few years. My best mentor and coach to date. Thanks, Andrew, for all the wisdom. Other coaches too.

NB* (Note bene; Note well.) Some people don't "want" to heal. Or are scared to start. I know people who probably won't heal, they don't want to change, they stay in their comfort zone even when it is painful. Because it's what they know. Because they honestly think that "pushing it down", "thinking positive" and "being grateful" will be enough. Because starting a vulnerable journey of facing the truth and looking within is bloody hard work. I know. You might too. Funnily though, once you start, the healing and more joy become addictive. Go figure! And the funny thing is, some people would like to feel better but just won't try the strategies, they are so set in their ways. Or they try them once but won't try a different way, they give up too quickly, or they are just too sceptical.

The answers are within you, yet you may need just a little help to find them.

Some of the strategies (ideas) here are simple, everyday practices that will improve your outlook. Things like journaling gratitudes and practising mindfulness. Looking at your exercise levels and improving them, understanding why exercise is so important. Trying new things for growth and learning. *"Stepping outside of your comfort zone, where the growth and learning occur."*

Deeper strategies will need a coach, counsellor, psychologist, whoever you think can help you (and I can help with that), maybe an online program, some reading, a weekend course, even You Tube. You decide how far you need or want to run with change. This book will introduce you to the ideas and where to look for the help you need.

More on who this book is for!

This book is for personal development, or self-help newbies (or dummies.) This was me just six or seven years ago. I didn't know what I didn't know. I knew there were answers out there, I just had to start my journey to find them. This book could be for you, your mother, sister, dad or brother, your kids, cousin, or friends. *Anyone really!* (Thanks, Ruth, for that catch phrase)

I really hope that families can use this book to help everyone in the family in these challenging times. (This is the name of another of my Facebook groups: *The Kids, Teens, and Families Whisperers: Support During Challenging Times.*) This is my superpower area. When I run a course, where we will go deeper on this subject, I want it to be for everyone. I also have a group I acquired from another coach, Doug, which has a great deal of personal development. It's called *The Confidence Academy*.

This book, I hope, could be the best gift you ever give to someone who needs this information.

This book has more ideas for personal development junkies (followers) like me. People who have started their journey and are adding tools to their toolkit!

This book is for people dealing with/reducing and accepting anxiety and depression.

I started my journey with a course with an amazing lady who had set up a gentle, polished, well packaged, mostly online course. She offered very basic strategies including yoga, breathing and basic personal development. Her course was, in my opinion, overpriced. So overpriced that I didn't tell anyone, not even a bestie housemate who kept asking. I did ask for some money back once I knew the industry better. I offered to halve the cost with her to no avail. She reminded me that I had written a good testimonial.

Be careful who you work with and do please "shop around". Don't get sucked in or stung like I was. But I now come from love and acceptance and try to let it go.

Then I found Andrew who was running *Anxiety Free Living* and the rest is history. I worked with people in Perth; Calvin and the *WILD* team who Andrew worked with in their *Self-Mastery*, then bounced from there into a course with Brett who worked with meditation; and, Roy, who worked in financial and personal goal setting. I signed up to attend the same college as Andrew and many other coaches I had started meeting. More about my journey later. Suffice to say that I met people of all ages and walks of life, from teens to over seventies.

This reminds me of a funny GIF that says something like: "I was doing this and that, then this happened, then that happened, and that's how I ended up under my bed looking at old photos." Story of my life. Some call it disorganised, scattered. Maybe I am working "in flow". I tried being organised once: worst three days of my life. (Joke drumbeat: da dum tish) Admit it, you said that out loud! I hope so!

Marco gave me a book once about embracing all your "stuff" and clutter. I loved that.

Whether you are goal driven or scattered, this book can help you find your way! But I suspect you will be here because you are feeling more scattered? Or someone in your life is?

The reading-level.

The reading level of this book is intended to be simple enough for teens and even older kids to read, maybe with the help of a caring adult. Or for parents to read and share the info with their kids. Because many families are struggling, especially with Covid, effects of climate change (fires, floods, and other weather events) and other world issues such as war.

As parents we can learn better ways to cope; let's share this with our kids, friends, and family.

Guarantee. (*Sort of.*)

(Please see the ***real disclaimer*** earlier in the book.)

I **HOPE** that if you practise these strategies regularly, you **WILL** feel better, day by day, week by week, month by month, year by year. They **MUST** become new habits, not just passing fads. Not like your gym membership that lasted from January to February. We are changing neural pathways here (links in the brain). You need to practise so much gratitude that it becomes automatic. Please read about gratitude under "J" for journaling as no amount of "doing gratitudes" can help you if you are still holding onto deep pain. You must resolve this with "I" for inner healing.

Commitment **You must exercise almost daily so it becomes part of your routine, as automatic as brushing your teeth. Try the other strategies and choose which ones work for you. Make a chart or print out mine from my group EMOJI: Find your happy face, write on a whiteboard, or make a vision board. If you have a family, this can be a family activity. Or do as a couple or as an individual. You can make a hard copy or do an online version, using Canva or similar.*

Again, I refer to the disclaimer here that if you have "baggage" or trauma, childhood wounds, you may need some deeper work to heal. I have had a truck (lorry) load and worked with many coaches to try different strategies.

So, in short, we have here a disclaimer that includes the fact that this is more than just "putting on a happy face" and we have a guarantee that this stuff works but you gotta "Do the work."

How long did it take you to learn to write or type? How long did it take you to learn to speak or walk? Fair enough you were just a small kid! Ok, then how long did it take you to learn to dance, sing, ride a bike, or cook meals?

This process; this journey will take time. Keep the book handy, join the Facebook group and hang out with us to learn more and see examples of success. I am not on all the other platforms as I just don't have the time or inclination to be everywhere. Some of my coaching mates are everywhere. I figure if you need me, you will find me. More info in *Contact Details*.

At this stage I don't want to have a VA (virtual assistant). I hope to need one when this book launches. I would ask a friend I think rather than someone "offshore". Ooo, I've just thought of someone! But I always want to keep messaging and interactions personal. There will be an accompanying program soon. I may even launch an app. In the words of my favourite Aussie comedian Dave Hughes, "Go me".

A conversation with Coach Dave:

In our EMOJI group, Dave made some comments and offered to chat. One day soon, we will have a bigger chat but for now, Dave says:" *Any technique may work for anybody at any time, but no technique will work for everybody every time.*"

Also: *"Progress is the result that occurs when we stop making trouble for ourselves. Get out of your own way and your self-correcting mental immune system will do its job. This is the Nature of Thought.*

Understand this and you can stop trying to think your way out of thought-generated problems. Understanding trumps techniques."

Thanks Dave, I think I understand. Just as I sometimes understand other coaches who I follow. And deeper level books I read.

I read these words by coaches that have way more experience and depth of understanding and I want to learn more. And I will in time.

Chapter 3.
EMOJI

EMOJI. A "Choose your own adventure" model; a "Dip in, try before you buy" model.

"*Choose your own Adventure*" were a series of children's books where you could take different paths to different endings, a fabulous idea. Kids loved them. Maybe a bit like some movies where the characters' outcomes are based on their choices. Hmm, a bit like life really.

EMOJI is a "choose your own adventure" model. Take meditation as an example. I never, ever thought I would be meditating. Now, I wish I had found it years ago. I do it most days, and I am keen to try many types of meditation. More on meditation under M for meditation. (Funny that.)

I did a beautiful five-day retreat in Byron Bay a couple of years ago to learn some different styles of meditation with Brett. I went by myself (in a friend's BMW, thanks Gekko) and stayed at the backpackers at the beach and felt like I was twenty-five again. There was a rope swing across the road on the way to the beach, hanging from a lovely tree, so then I felt twelve again! I was ready to move there and hang with the hippies and learn surfing, which I did with a friend, Angelica, one weekend. We bought clothes from young woman at a garage sale (yard sale) across the road from the backpackers.

At the meditation retreat we told our stories first to let go of deep pain, then we tried so many different meditations to music, candles, silent meditation, breathwork, the lot! We got better at it each day. We learned a great deal about meditation, which you can learn in Brett's book, *Awaken*, see *Resources*. Thanks Brett.

Another friend, Karen, and I attended a weekend yoga camp, staying in "dongas" (portable cabins), eating vegetarian food, drinking water and herbal tea and we had a blast. Confession: We did sneak up town for a coffee one time though.

I am in meditation groups that I love. I used to enjoy meditating to music, but at the moment, I like 10-minute guided meditations with a purpose, which my good friend, Karen, (from the yoga camp) recommended to me. My partner, Frank, a fairly "blokey" bloke, who never meditated until I introduced him to it, likes to be alone and just be quiet. Working on the breath. He now watches You Tube videos on Sadguru, an Indian Yogi with so much wisdom. There are many others. My daughter, Lisa, is (finally) meditating; the free class she attends uses chants for focus, like a mantra. We recently made jokes about Sat Nam (a mantra) and her old mate Govinda. (Krishna, Google to find out more.)

A case study, James. One of my meditation groups uses a different type of meditation, known as *Frequency Healing* or *Human Re-Engineering* where we focus on something in the room, and we even focus on our internal organs. I have watched the transformations of the leader of this group, James, who has become a good friend and mentor, and listened to the stories of his mentor, Mas, who had near death experiences which led him to meditation; so powerful.

A Case Study, Paul. Another coaching friend, Paul, has written a free e-book on meditation. He has one hundred and fifty-five thousand followers on Facebook alone. People are looking for wisdom, peace and even spirituality. I recently interviewed him. He was bullied as a child and always felt different. He over- ate in his youth and young adulthood and had a weight problem. Then he studied some styles of coaching and now he looks amazingly fit and healthy, coaches people and teaches meditation. What an inspiring transformation. Paul has kindly written the foreword for this book. Thanks Paul.

We are even teaching kids in schools now to meditate, and the results are wonderful! I have read studies and seen it for myself. The first time I was teaching in a school and the meditation music came on after break, I cried with happiness.

I cried with happiness when I first saw them teaching meditation in schools. Kids need this big time; we all do!

So, you see, something as simple as Meditation, just one strategy in this model, can have so many avenues or paths. In marketing they say, "points of entry". More on meditation and mindfulness in the M chapters.

*The best part is that YOU get to choose what you like. What works for you. If you come into our EMOJI Facebook group, EMOJI: Find your happy face! Shared strategies for wellness and joy! (This name may change but you will find us.) You can share ideas and learn from others. So, sit back, relax, and enjoy the ride. You can dip in or read from cover to cover. You choose! Be sure to keep your copy to dip into any time.

*Please buy a copy for anyone in your life who needs this work!

*Use the index at the back of the book to find specific topics.

☺

Chapter 4.
Anxiety and Depression

These are my thoughts on anxiety and depression.

Anxiety and depression are chemical, but WE make the chemicals. **Sharon Chemello.**

The best quote I ever posted on Facebook was "Anxiety and depression are chemical, but WE make the chemicals." It came to me in a blinding flash one day after "doing the work" for a couple of years. Working with coaches; reading and doing courses. Apart from "happy snaps", it was my most popular post. Because most of my friends and followers have "done the work".

When I first experienced early morning panic attacks and generalised anxiety, which wore me down and led to severe post-natal depression, I had no idea! I had always been a worrier and would lose sleep worrying. I had a truck load of childhood issues and all the universal fears: *not being worthy, or good enough*; *not feeling loved, and not belonging. Also: fear of trusting and surrendering, (aligns with not being worthy or good enough) abandonment and separation (not belonging).*

I had so much fear and didn't know what to do. I had no idea where to find the journey or where to start.

We don't know what we don't know.

As we say in coaching: "I didn't know what I didn't know". I was certainly looking for answers until someone snapped at me "You're always looking for answers!", so then I did it sneakily. I went to many alternate health practitioners and read books. I was on Facebook all the time, yet I didn't even know you could find personal development there. I was mostly scrolling through friends' holiday snaps and chatting with old school mates. Until one day after my separation, an ad came up for a personal development coach.

I must have "told" the algorithm that I was looking at this kind of stuff. I had a phone call with the coach who specialised in women who felt stuck and next thing I am forking out thousands of dollars to take her mostly online course with a few one-on-one calls and group calls. I later contacted her to say I had more experience in the industry and now knew her course was overpriced and suggested that maybe she was taking advantage of separated and divorced women, or women with anxiety and depression? That maybe we could halve the price. She cited the great review I had given her and stood firm. So, my learning experience and advice is, please "shop around" and don't rush into coaching. I have also learned how to let go and come from love more than fear. See it as growth and learning.

Choose a coach who is experienced and works with you to achieve the outcomes you want and need, not what they want. What you first go to see them for, may change too. There are many group coaching programs now, which can be a great starting place. Then you can decide if you want to work one on one with the coach.

I have many, many coaching friends working with anxiety and depression and there are free programs and fairly priced programs everywhere.

Anxiety and depression have so many definitions. Anxiety is technically the flight, fright, or freeze response left over (still in our reptilian brain) from our cave man days, where we had to run from danger. The problem is, as you will hear coaches say, that there are no dinosaurs or sabre tooth tigers to run from, yet we still have the anxiety. (Perhaps someone in your life is as scary as one of these creatures, but you can learn to deal with them with help.)

Some say depression is lack of purpose. That anxiety is worrying about the future and depression is worrying about the past. I think it's much more.

There are clinical definitions. Reduced serotonin, so antidepressants are prescribed. There are anti-anxiety meds and depression meds galore. Big pharma is cleaning up! Statistics are high, especially during Covid and other challenging times. There are lots of other conditions; Bipolar, PTSD, (Post traumatic stress syndrome) and more. People with ADHD and on the Autism Spectrum often have accompanying anxiety and/ or depression conditions. People with disabilities often do. People who have chronic illness often do.

> *We are overprescribing, masking symptoms, and not looking enough into alternatives. We need healing and help to find our happy face, naturally. Using all the strategies in EMOJI and others that work for you.* **Sharon Chemello.**

I don't plan to debate medications here. Suffice to say, I don't think I would be here without them. However, we have many more tools at our disposal and should be using those! Medication or not, people need support and strategies for wellness. The medications are very hard to come off, I know firsthand. But all the wellness ideas in this book are the way to do it. Maybe supported by herbal remedies, or some say CBD oil. *Please do your own research.*

After the online course for women that I did, I found a great group to study and train with, from Perth. They teach personal development and coaching skills. Within six months of training with them for a long weekend and various online courses, especially my best mentor who worked in anxiety, I found myself on the team "crewing" for them, supporting others and I suddenly realised how far I had come in six months. But you gotta "do the work"; there is no magic pill.

I still had a lot of anxiety. Much of it was from childhood, "limiting beliefs" (another coaching term) and much from the grief of separation and divorce and losing my family unit. A great deal of shame and guilt, and I was still drinking at this point; about the worst thing for someone with anxiety and depression. More about alcohol and addictions under O for "Own your Shizzle." I did however find a coach for addiction, Tom, and continued with the anxiety coach, Andrew.

"I can cure your anxiety and depression in 10 days!"

Around this time, the coach from Perth, Calvin, made a huge, bold statement on Facebook, that he could help people out of anxiety and depression and off medications in ten days. Ok, maybe he exaggerated a tad, yet I now understand his sentiments. At the time, there was a huge backlash and I joined in by saying that perhaps he had never experienced or witnessed debilitating anxiety and depression. I know first-hand that many of his strategies are helpful, yet it was too big a call.

I was triggered and I "bit" hard! However, ever curious, and open minded, *DOUBT NOTHING,* I did more work with their group and even went to Bali with them. That's how I met the meditation coach, Brett, who also does couples and relationship work with his partner Marie; and a financial and personal development coach, Roy, in his seventies, who I went to the Hunter Valley with. This is how people like me spend so much time and money on personal development.

You can find so much online for free. As I write this, two big American personal development guys, Tony Robbins and Dean Graziosi are wrapping up a free five-day challenge. With of course, an option to buy another program. Some of these courses seriously change lives. They can be a starting point.

*Follow *The Happiness Co* with Julian Pace in Australia. Follow *I am Enough Coaching* with Steve Barker. Follow Andrew Pearce, or *WILD* with Calvin Coyles. I will mention many others I like in the *Resources.*

I didn't understand what the coach from Perth was saying, yet I do now, and I thank him and all my other coaches. I am currently being mentored by my amazing publishing coach, Emma, and at the same time, working with Andrew. I am in a coaching group with Steve called *I am Enough Academy*. I recently worked with a couple of coaches, they were in New Zealand, now back in Bali, Caleb and Donna, who teach human behaviour and sales. I am learning so much about myself and healing more parts of me, letting go of old stories, habits, and beliefs. I've had a nutrition coach, Matty and been in his program *Ultimate Energy Upgrade* and his *Consistency Club*.

So, anxiety and depression are real and can be debilitating. I've reached rock bottom a few times in my life, and it was the love of my kids, family members and friends, that kept me going. And coaches and their teachings. I'm here for a reason and part of that is to teach this stuff!

Always, always reach out. See *Resources*.

There is so much you can do to heal and to feel better, calmer, and happier. EMOJI has all the strategies that worked for me and many people I know.

Chapter 5.
Modalities, Strategies, Ideas.

> The number of modalities is infinite.
> Keep your mind open.

The number of modalities, strategies and ideas out there is infinite with something new coming up all the time. People playing with existing modalities and tweaking them, often with huge success. One of my goals in life is to fulfil my bucket list of activities. I have tried surfing, skateboarding, Latin dance, skydiving and more. I also have a bucket list of healing and transformational modalities I am trying. You just never know what may work for you or help others you meet.

An example of keeping an open mind. For years I suffered with a bad knee, from sport as a teen. The X-ray said the knee was "corrugated". The corrugations were causing inflammation which caused pain. I was offered an operation to "sand" the corrugations smooth, anti-inflammatory drugs for possibly the rest of my days, or maybe I could try acupuncture. I was lucky to have a progressive GP (general practitioner or doctor) to suggest this.

There is something about the acupuncture needles being a foreign body, which sends our body into defence mode, thereby reducing the inflammation. Three sessions later, I haven't had any trouble with the knee at all. That was about 30 years ago. I recently asked my acupuncturist, Chris, why is it permanent? He said, it isn't always, but if it flares up again, just have more acupuncture. Simple. Acupuncture also helped heal my recuring sinus. That and a daily saltwater flush which I learned from my holistic acupuncturist Chris. Thanks Chris.

From this experience and others, I learned to keep my mind open. Whilst other friends and family popped pills for ailments, I looked for alternatives and answers. I have found so many.

React vs Respond. An example about Basil.

As I write this, Basil the Fawlty Dog, now renamed by a coaching friend and essential oils advocate, Lisa, as Basil the Brilliant; is driving me nuts, tossing a ball under a cupboard, getting it stuck and then whining until I get down on the floor (sore knee from my recent melanoma operation and all) to retrieve the ball. I just did that, four times, cursing and swearing and threatening to put him outside. Reacting rather than responding. Thinking I may have to go get a long piece of timber for retrieval. Knowing he is trying to get my attention, like a small child. Thinking, "I just sat down to write, and you do this? You are soooo annoying Basil." But wait? How could I respond? What could I do differently? *Get curious or observe.*

Einstein said if we keep doing the same thing and expect a different result, this is the definition of insanity!

I finally stopped reacting and found an old towel to roll up and place at the base of the cupboard to prevent the ball going under. Problem solved! Everybody happy. I may even buy a door sausage. Done.

* How can you respond rather than react to things that happen to you? Many coaches say, "Life is not happening to you, it's happening FOR you!" Rhonda Byrne, The Secret. Often quoted by gurus like Tony Robbins.

The problem might not be big enough!

One of my coaches, Tom, who I worked with for addiction to alcohol, often says "The problem is not big enough" if you know what to do and don't do it. Amen to that. I spent years sleeping badly, eating sugar, and taking antidepressants. Self-sabotaging to the nth degree, dating badly and writing angry letters. Staying up late on social media, or looking at holidays or real estate. Dreaming about life changes but not taking real action.

Is this you or someone you love?

Staying in bed in the morning until the last possible minute then racing to work and running late. Then crying and super anxious.

ALMOST EVERY MORNING!

Go figure! If this is you, you're in the right place! Let's begin here. And please reach out if you need help. I will be setting up a program to accompany the book. Start by joining the group for free. My contact details will be in the back of this book, along with testimonials from clients I have worked with. These are also mini case studies.

Doubt nothing!

I will be saying this, many times in this book. I have said "Keep an open mind" and I want to say it stronger and say, DOUBT NOTHING! Things I doubted years ago have become my most powerful tools. A Reiki session with Yvonne had me shaking. Yvonne also coached me through some childhood trauma, and it was so powerful. Acupuncture with David cured my aching knee. Acupuncture with Chris cured my recurring sinus and throat infections. The vibrations of the crystal bowls with Tracey, had me crying, releasing, and a funny tummy for days. As she predicted could happen. E for energy!

Don't get me started on meditation and some of the amazing overwhelming feelings and results I've had. I've had some very spiritual experiences in life, and the number just increases with the studies and learnings.

Frank loves watching videos on UFOs, (now termed UAPs: Unidentified Aerial Phenomena.) I am watching a few and have totally changed my beliefs. There is now a great deal of evidence, some of which has been long hidden from us.

The power of the subconscious is amazing, I am also very interested in dream interpretation and the power of dreams. One to study soon. And maybe help people see the power of their subconscious and what it's teaching us.

Let's go a little woo woo and 'raise your vibration'.

Have you heard about raising your vibration? People like Dr Bruce Lipton and David Hawkins, some call it quantum physics, and some don't like the use of this terminology. Because the original quantum physics or quantum mechanics is a different type of science. Raising your vibration is an accepted terminology by many. The theory is that we all have frequencies, like atoms. That we can raise our vibration by using strategies such as many mentioned in this book. David Hawkins produced a scale of vibrations where emotions such as fear, guilt and shame are at low levels of vibration; acceptance and love are around the middle; and joy and enlightenment are at the top of the scale. If you Google "*raising your vibration*" you can find out more.

A little on morning and evening rituals.

Many people use a morning, evening, or bedtime ritual every day. I will speak more to this in E for evening and M for morning. Many famous people like Oprah, Tony Robbins and Richard Branson swear by these rituals. Some get up at early hours of the day before daylight to engage in rituals, to fit them into their day and start their day well. They call this "setting up your day for success" and similar names. I really admire these people. It's not something I do well, but I am working on it. I'm better in the summer months!

What about you?

The same applies in the evening maybe before dinner or after dinner, before bed. The rituals can have any number of parts to them.

You can set up an area, or even a shrine or altar as they do in some cultures. This can be very creative, calming, and powerful. It could be a fun activity to design with a partner, friend, housemate, or family. In Catholic schools, we have a prayer table. Maybe something like that in your home, a small area where you could place spiritual items. A set of shelves even.

Sustainable Crusaders.

Frank and I have a group called *Sustainable Crusaders* on Facebook and Instagram, maybe even Tik Tok soon! Watch this space! Our You Tube channel is *Sustainable Crusaders AUS Travels*. We started as *Crusaders Against Plastic* and over time we have added more information on general sustainability. Because it's more than just plastic. Whilst we reduce our plastic at home, buy less plastic, do beach clean-ups, and live sustainably, we are also looking at things like clothing, cooking, building, and vege gardens.

We are now adding lifestyle factors such as nutrition, exercise, relationships, emotional management, even healing trauma and childhood wounds to become more mentally and physically sustainable.

We will be travelling a lap of Australia in a year from now and teaching sustainability. More on this under M for mission.

Postscript: The vege patches are ready to go now and I can't tell you the joy that brings me!

I recently met a mum, with two kids, in Aldi Supermarket, complaining about the cost of lettuce. I was a bit passive aggressive and said, "Time for a vege patch." As if I was brilliant, she said "That's a good idea!" *We have lost our roots! (Sad face)*

Chapter 6.
E

Exercise	Energy	Emotion	Evolving
Enthusiasm	Earthing	Experiences	Excitement
EFT (Emotional Freedom Technique – Tapping)			Evening Rituals
Expectations	Empathy	Experiment	

Let's look at some of these. This is not a complete list, it is some of my own ideas from my training and reading and some of the suggestions provided to me, by members of my group. There are more. Can you think of others? Leave a comment in the group and use the notes section at the end of the chapter.

Exercise.

Exercise has literally saved my life! I have always known the benefits of exercise and done many forms of exercise for most of my life. I studied a fitness certificate to further my knowledge. I have taught aerobics, group fitness and aqua aerobics. I've done yoga, Pilates, and gym. Since my separation, I've done more yoga, gym, and boot camp. I've learned to surf and skateboard, stand up paddle board and more.

Whenever I've had anxiety and depression, I've walked most mornings, to take the edge off, get fresh air and produce the happy chemicals. Endorphins, happy chemicals and hormones such as dopamine and serotonin. Getting out into the fresh air and sunshine gives us Vitamin D, which helps to lift your mood. Listening to the birds and being mindful as we walk around our neighbourhood, at the beach, or in a park, can offer real benefits. It's often the last thing you feel like doing, but if you do it anyway and make it a new habit, the benefits will appear.

"Feel the fear and do it anyway." Or the Nike slogan, "Just do it."

Coach Steve told us about a lady who just started by getting off the couch, then walked around the couch, then went outside, then around the block. Wow!

Exercise can boost immunity and lower "stress" or "angry" chemicals like cortisol and sometimes even adrenaline which comes with anxiety. It can even increase libido ("feeling loving" for the kids reading.) Exercise can help us sleep and relax.

Exercise can help with brain function, muscle development, bone density (making bones stronger), building confidence, strength, and flexibility. For some, exercise is the most important part of EMOJI. Yoga and Pilates are especially good for strength and flexibility. And Yoga is preparation for meditation.

As I write this, I have found research which shows that exercise helps with cancer healing.

For families: Set up a family exercise program, chat about what kinds of exercise everyone likes and start doing them one at a time. I used to simply have a rule that my kids had to spend thirty minutes outside after school. (They also had to do some jobs or chores each day.) When you are struggling to convince kids to commit to things, remember "It's our job as parents to help them be better people and to set up good habits." If you have family rules that you stick to, the consistency becomes the norm. Ignore the groans. And for kids reading this, exercise will help you with EVERYTHING! It even helps your brain function.

Energy

How we produce or create energy is vital information. What sort of things make good energy? What we eat and drink for starters. Protein and good fats. Vegetables and some (less) carbohydrates. Water,

water, water! Cow's milk, or other animals, nut milk (or nut liquid), or coconut. (Just be sure to check with your nutritionist or do some research about the various types.) Kombucha (fermented drink with probiotics). Fermented food such as sauerkraut and kimchi (fermented cabbage and other ingredients.) Exercise gives us more energy, as we get fitter. Mindfulness and meditation (coming in M) can create energy. Healing ourselves emotionally, can create more energy as we let go of stress.

I am working with a nutrition coach, Matty, who runs a group for busy working women. I am now in his *Consistency Club* after doing his *UEU, Ultimate Energy Upgrade*. I have learned so much about creating energy in my body and what depletes energy, like sugar, which Matty says is as addictive as heroin, cocaine and caffeine.

Energy can be so much more. Yin and Yang, masculine and feminine energies. Shiva and Shakti. The Chakras. Quantum Physics. These are all areas to explore and learn more, some may suit you, some may not. You've possibly heard of many of these areas of energy. They can all be powerful areas of growth and healing.

* Google these areas to learn more! I am learning about all of these. Ask me for places to go!

DISC model. A model I see being used a great deal lately is the DISC model of behaviour types and energies. D is for dominant, I is for influencer, S is for stable and C is for compliant. There are many traits for each type. There are other energy type models as well. Understanding energies can help communication, relationships, and businesses.

Some of this Energy area is often debated as the mainstream meets the "woo woo" (spiritual). But as I say, keep your mind open, doubt nothing!

I am here to tell you that as true as I sit here, I have had some major "woo woo" experiences myself. I have felt things that have been trapped in my subconscious, I have felt beyond this dimension or realm, I have felt physical reactions to treatments and modalities. I have fallen asleep during some really heavy emotional work, because my subconscious was trying to protect me.

I've had some spiritual experiences during meditation. And yesterday as I was writing this, Frank gave me a small old item, a silver thimble for protecting fingers when sewing. He found it and thought I would like it, and I suddenly had the most amazing connection to my maternal grandmother which I've never had before. She died when I was almost three and I had felt like I didn't remember much about her, yet now I believe there is much more in my subconscious.

I have had some repressed memories triggered by events in my life. I know with absolute certainty about this. I am fascinated by our dreams and what they represent and have done some studies in this area and enjoy dream analysis. I am becoming quite good at this.

I have never been one to look for these things. I did want to believe in the universe looking out for us and providing things when we need them, yet I am fairly logical and believe that we can take action and make things happen. And then, people and events come into my life just when I need them, and you know....

My coach and mentor Andrew has even "deeper" (different) beliefs. I teach in Catholic schools where people I work with have stronger beliefs than me. I retain an open mind and...

Doubt nothing. We don't know what we don't know. There is much out there we don't understand and can learn about if we choose.

This is all energy.

On nutrition and gut health.

There are many coaches teaching this stuff. I work with Matty, and I have had some help from others such as Leanne and Lisa W. Many believe that the gut health affects all other areas of our health including mental health. Hence my earlier statement on anxiety and depression that we make the chemicals. We are learning the value of nutrition for healing cancer, for many health conditions and even things like ADHD. My coaching friend, Lillian, and her naturopath son Nate, speak to this in great depth in their program *The Nurtured Heart Approach*. Perfect for families and even relationships.

Sleep is vital in creating energy. Most people need about seven or eight hours sleep a night. I worked with a Melbourne psychologist, David, who created a sleep program, to get his program onto Facebook. I had read the program twenty years ago when I had severe post-natal depression, and a counsellor gave a copy to me. It helped save my life! For twenty years I planned to contact the doctor, to thank him and offer to help market the program, yet life always got in the way. During Covid 2020, I finally did.

Sleep repairs the body and the mind, helps with anxiety and depression and immunity. It allows our body and brain time to repair. Some studies are now showing the importance of sleep for healing and prevention of illnesses such as dementia. I'm in. (Matty also has news on mushrooms and dementia.)

Message me if you'd like help with sleep. Doctor David's program, *Sleep Better without Drugs* is a four-to-six-week program with a success rate in the high eighties. Of the people who weren't successful, many did not allow the full four to six weeks. When it was at its height, the program sold over twenty thousand copies. Second time around was not as successful as the market is saturated. And David believes it needs to be promoted through general practitioners, psychologists, and counsellors.

The program is on Facebook and contains many videos and posts to help you sleep, before even buying the program. I know other coaches who also specialise in sleep. See *Resources* at the back of the book for further information.

Good sleep requires things such as catching the wave of sleep, the ultradian rhythm (the sixty-to-ninety-minute cycle of sleep) which Doctor David explains simply. Waking up at the same time each day. Turning off screens an hour before bed. Not eating after dinner. A healthy diet, exercise, and relaxation activities. Reduced substances such as alcohol, nicotine, and caffeine. Just like other parts of EMOJI, none of this is rocket science, it's stuff we may already know, yet we need to make it more conscious and proactive.

Matty, the nutrition coach and another coach, Sveti, also teach about sleep. As do many other coaches and no doubt psychologists and counsellors.

See also *Evening Ritual*, for more ways to create good sleep and rest.

For families: Explain all of this to kids as simply as possible. Use nutrition charts on the fridge, I just received one from my doctor, use sleep meditations for kids and teens. Have family discussions, use this book for stimulus. Ask kids what they think. How often do we get caught up with what the teacher said, or what Johnny did. Plan to extend the dinner time discussions to wellness ideas.

Emotions.

EMOJI is over 50 ideas for overcoming anxiety and finding your happy face. Emotions are neither good nor bad, they just *are*. Just like emojis. Emotions can teach us if we listen.

As one mentor and coach, Andrew says, imagine a tennis ball in a jar of water. The tennis ball is your emotions which we shut down over and over, rather than face them and deal with them. I use his analogy/demonstration often with clients, especially kids and teens. I bought a small plastic fishbowl and use old tennis balls. One is broken which I say is because it was pushed down too much (which is actually true). I colour the water blue for effect. This is a great strategy to use with your kids and teens.

All over the personal development, self-help, wellness and mental health industry and the internet, are coaches, counsellors and psychologists that can help you with healing emotions. There are powerful modalities, such as NLP *(neuro linguistic programming)*, CBT *(cognitive behaviour therapy)*, hypnosis, Reiki, Inner Child Therapy and more! I will speak more to EFT (Emotional Freedom Technique) or "Tapping," and I recently had some sessions of Quantum Healing Hypnosis Technique with a practitioner, Paul, who follows and studied with Delores Cannon's work. This is a technique that uses story and hypnosis. There are many other therapies.

Case Study: Andrew. I am currently doing another course with my favourite coach and mentor, Andrew. I started with him about five years back in a group about reducing anxiety. He had social anxiety and worked at a supermarket. He was going to study psychology then decided on coaching. He is an avid reader of very high-level modern-day philosophers such as Eckhardt Tolle and David Hawkins.

I have done several courses with Andrew, on inner flow and shadow work as it's sometimes called, and his recent offering and title of his book, *Awaken*. I've had some amazing transformations and awareness. I just stopped writing for a moment, to sign up for some one-on-one coaching with him. *Taking action!* At the time of editing, this work is creating the shifts I've been looking for. *Postscript: This work and the transformations I have made are next level.*

*If you have some stuff you are hanging onto, or need help to uncover why you self-sabotage, why emotions are so strong, or you know you need healing, please find a coach, counsellor or psychologist. I cannot urge you strongly enough. I am a very different person to the one I was five years ago. I can handle almost anything, or anyone now; I welcome constructive feedback (mostly) willingly and I can let go of so many emotions I would previously hang onto for days or weeks. I am setting boundaries and people pleasing and apologising less.

Many believe that trauma is stored in our body, like stress. I think we all know that we often get sick when we are tired, run down and stressed.

I am happy to report that in schools now, we are teaching kids about emotions and how to deal with them. At my current base school, we use an amazing program called *Reboot*, which teaches kids how to recognise their emotions and self-regulate when they are upset. I am studying with an American company who teaches similar. Another coaching friend, Lillian, teaches a method called *The Nurtured Heart Approach*, which helps parents and kids work together in a positive way. It's based on the work of Howard Glasser, an American Psychologist. Lillian's son helps as a naturopath with nutrition and environmental concerns.

Emotions can be classified as good or bad, positive, and negative, and many see this as unhelpful, they believe we are better to see all emotions as useful. Get curious about what they are teaching us. Some classify them as resourceful and unresourceful. Some welcome all emotions and teach us how to work with them for greater awareness. Many of our emotions are from our childhood, particularly during formative years, zero to seven. The more we learn about our inner child, the more we understand human behaviour of ourselves and others. Many of my coaching friends teach about emotions. One, Angela, does a week-by-week breakdown and explanation. What each emotion is and how it manifests or plays out in life. This information is gold! Then we can watch our family and friends with curiosity and even a court case with famous actors with new perspectives. Another coaching mate, Corey, has just released a stand-up spiral book called *The Little Book of BIG Emotions*.

We are all children, the sooner we learn and accept that, the easier life becomes. **Sharon Chemello.**

As I am finishing this part on emotions and am chatting with Frank, he reminds me that we sat at a café recently, writing some *Three Rs on Sustainable Relationships* as part of our *Sustainable Crusaders*. *Resilience, Revival (of the spark) and Respect.* I put this to my group and others added more. I added *Reframe*. Emma W suggests *Reflect, Reframe and Relate*. Lillian in her Nurtured Heart Approach uses *Reset*. At my school we use *Reboot*.

Frank also adds that love and tenderness should be part of emotions. What a keeper hey? Frank has come a long way in his journey too.

I am reminded of the five love languages and how they support our emotional needs. Gary Chapman wrote a book called *The Five Love Languages*: words of affirmation, physical touch, acts of service, gifts, and quality time.

Chapman's books are wonderful for couples, families, and individuals.

For Families: Corey's book, The Little Book of BIG Emotions, could be a great starting point. Make the tennis ball and jar prop. Discuss emotions over dinner. "How did you feel when....". Allow kids to get angry or cry. See Stephanie's work for small kids Yolande's work for teens, Lillian too (all in Resources.)

Empathy.

The ability to understand and share the feelings of another. (Oxford)

According to psychologists, there are three components: cognitive, emotional, and compassionate.

Empathy can be nurtured, or taught, too. In my teaching I often find myself teaching kids empathy. Empathy is often described as "walking in another's shoes." Understanding how someone feels. More than sympathy. Sympathy is understanding from your own perspective. Imagining or knowing how something would feel for another. Empathy goes beyond, feeling from their perspective. Empathy is a wonderful skill to have. It can help you see beyond your own problems. Not to dismiss your problems, but to understand the pain of others.

Nas Yassin, from Nas Daily, says we should learn to understand each other's *fight language* just as we do *love languages*. One person might want to solve the conflict as soon as possible, the other might want to think for a while. Understanding and empathising with the other can help.

For families: Follow families' coaches such as those mentioned and in Resources for more info. Work with kids and teens on empathy. Discuss feelings of your own and others. Use situations as they arise to teach empathy. Maybe not right away, but sometime later, maybe after everyone has calmed down.

EFT (Emotional Freedom Technique) or "Tapping."

I first learned this technique from an amazing family friend, Marie, who I knew when I was a teen. She knew my family and our challenges. She became a counsellor and practised hypnosis. I ran into her husband, Anthony, at the shops (mall) and told him about some major life challenges I was having, and he said, "Come and see Marie." Thanks so much Anthony, ever grateful. As well as some wonderful counselling, Marie showed me Tapping, EFT, Emotional Freedom Technique, and I have learned a whole lot more since.

EFT is defined as a treatment for emotional and physical pain. It has been proven to help with anxiety and other mental health issues. There are "tapping points" on the body, usually bony areas. Whilst tapping, we use affirmations or statements. I have personally found it highly beneficial. I met another practitioner recently and we did some live tapping on Facebook, helping me with a limiting belief. Sue calls her technique by another name. (See *Resources.*)

I have taught many people about Tapping. I have found it very powerful. I believe that the Tapping takes the affirmation into the body and subconscious. You use the affirmations regularly, which becomes a habit, which "sticks". When I was slowly giving up alcohol with my amazing coach Tom, I often said "Did a silly thing, we all do silly things, I love and respect myself anyway." I have used this for any self-sabotage "mistakes."

There are Facebook and other social media groups who teach Tapping. There are courses, just Google. Pat, who taught me Spiral, a methodology explained further in other parts of the book, teaches a method for Tapping for kids using a teddy bear.

For families: There are many places on the internet for tapping with kids and others for adults. Ask me if you need help.

Evening Ritual.

As mentioned in the introduction, morning and evening rituals can change your life. Evening ritual can be after dinner or before bed for best results. Or it could be in the late afternoon or evening. It can include some exercise and meditation and anything you wish to add. We all know to turn off screens well before bedtime. And we know the importance of sleep for resting our minds and bodies and allowing our bodies to repair and heal.

I personally love a bedtime ritual. It could be anything from watching a Sadhguru video which we often do here at home, to some stretches, gratitudes (See J for Journaling), affirmations, a quiet or musical meditation and some herbal tea. Frank and I buy an herbal tea mixture from our local health food shop where they know which ingredients to include such as Valerian, (not the best smell but very effective) Marshmallow Root, Camomile, and other restful herbs. We keep it in a big jar and use a coffee plunger. (But you can also buy tea bags, we just prefer to reduce the small amounts of plastic often in tea bags.) We set two alarms, one to get ready for bed and one to go to bed after a warm shower. And of course, cleaning our teeth. Sometimes I add in some music, meditation, mental gratitudes, stretches. I pop essential oils in the diffuser or on the pillow or pulse points on the body.

Sometimes, I have an early evening ritual with a walk at the beach, some stretches and meditation, and a nice kombucha while listening to music and making dinner. You can make your ritual whatever you like and as mentioned in the intro, even have a special space. Some cultures of course have a shrine or altar. This is something you can do. I used to have a shrine to Yoda at my townhouse where I had heaps of pop culture. Karen and I meet at the beach every Wednesday afternoon and do stretches, personal development and meditation. This is our weekly ritual. It is really important to us both. You could find a friend or family member and do this once a week.

For families: Set up rituals with your kids. Decide together what to include. Make charts, or a vision board. (See Appendix.) Set up a nice area, table, shrine, or altar. Kids love this sort of thing. They can bring things to the table. A pet rock, shell, candle, toy, photo, or book.

Earthing or grounding.

Another E strategy I love is E for earthing, sometimes called grounding. Walking barefoot on grass, sand, soil, mulch, pebbles, rocks, or in water. It is a wonderful sensory experience; one we lost a long time ago when shoes were invented. It can take you back to your roots, for some. Or it can just be a fun, "grounding" experience. You can research this strategy online. It can be very powerful. One of my friends, Noel, was very much into it and even had a wire from his bed to the ground below. *Remember: doubt nothing.* Some of us didn't believe in UFOs until recently. Some of us still won't and that's ok. Some of us believe in Santa Claus and fairies. Or the spirit of....

For families: Take everyone somewhere and go barefoot! Encourage barefoot grounding and earthing. And please hug a tree for me! Have you ever done that? Time to start!

Evolving

As I write this book, I add a new idea every day! Some of them seem so obvious. Coach Harry does an *evening evolution*, with valuable info for change and personal development. I just met a new coach from the same coaching college and his business name is *Evolve with Coach Ross*. I'm jealous of that one!

For families: Discuss evolution and ask kids and teens "How can we evolve?" "How can we make our family life better, what can we do to help the planet? To make the world a better place?"

Experiment and Explore

Experiment with and explore the ideas in this book and others you will find once you've started your journey.

Other E strategies.

Eat that Frog. Brian Tracy, a Canadian "Guru", talks about doing a hard thing first, rather than putting it off. As hard as eating a frog. I have a frog fridge magnet on my desk to remind me. But then Frank says "Pick the low hanging fruit first. Some days this works better! *Choose your own adventure.*

Empowerment. Ego. Encouragement.

What could you add here in the notes section? Choose your own adventure.

There are many books on Ego and how it plays out in our lives. Ego can protect us or cause sabotage. Ego is a whole other subject!

Just as I am finishing on this book draft, I listen to coach Steve's podcast, *Inner Work,* and he is talking about dealing with conflict and mentions the three Es. *Explain, Explore and Empower.* I think today I will just sit and write and not listen to or look at social media, or this book will never end! Which is a good thing!

Strategies for wellness, communication and connection are everywhere! Yippee!

***Please post more ideas in the group on Facebook any time to add to the model, we love it!*

Notes For E.

Chapter 7.
M

Mindfulness	Meditation	Manifestation	Music	Mission
Morning rituals	Mastery	Motivation	Massage	
Musings	Magic	Movement		

Let's look at some of these. This is not a complete list, it is some of my own from my training and reading and some of the suggestions provided to me, by members of my group. There are more. Can you think of others? Leave a comment in the group and use the notes section at the end of the chapter.

Mindfulness

What is mindfulness?

We hear a lot about mindfulness, in schools, and in personal development. A good friend of mine since childhood was going to mindfulness classes one night a week as I was starting my journey. This was a regular hard-working guy, running his own business, with an open mind, who knew he needed help with his thinking. He had a great deal of stress in his life and like me, was drinking to "cope."

Is this you or someone you love? Please share this work!

I went and bought a book on mindfulness to understand more. Wow! Such a simple yet effective strategy. I thank my friend for helping me get started. This led to an eight-week course with an amazing mindfulness teacher in Brisbane. Manish was born in India and his family practised meditation and mindfulness as Hindus. They moved to California, and he studied science. He worked in his field yet noticed more and more that people were stressed and not mindful of things in their everyday world that could slow down their thoughts and create some inner peace. He began studying meditation and teaching mindfulness which is a very simple version. When I Googled just now to get the spelling of his name right, I found numerous studies about the positive benefits of mindfulness. This also applies to Meditation and Gratitude, which I've included under J for Journaling.

We started by breathing slowly, eating a grape, and using the five senses to feel, (touch) taste, see, hear, and smell. We walked outside on the grass with bare feet, this is often called earthing or grounding, included under E for Earthing.

We looked at the history of meditation and mindfulness and tried many exercises. It was a wonderful way to spend eight nights with like-minded people in an old sailing club hall by the river. I guess it was really the start of my journey.

Mindfulness can be as simple as using the five senses, what can I see, hear, smell, touch, and taste? This is a great way to teach mindfulness to kids.

Here's what Manish' webpage says: "*One of the ways to deal with uncertainty in today's social climate is to cultivate mindfulness. Learn simple meditation exercises to incorporate inner peace, calm and wellbeing into your daily life. Seek out your inner strength to stay balanced and be present for those around you – especially during these challenging times.*"

For families: Google mindfulness ideas for kids and teens, or just start by using the five senses. Go on mindfulness walks and notice things. Encourage this. Encourage them to come home from school, work or university/college and tell you three things they noticed today and how it made them feel. Enrol your family in a mindfulness course, suitable for kids. Look around! Allow them to take photos and make an album or a chart. I will be running a course next year. Maybe a short "taster" course late this year.

Meditation.

Some say meditation is all about the breath. Breathwork is also a "thing." You can learn breathwork in so many ways. Some say meditation is stillness. Peace and calming the mind.

Karen says "*It sets me up calmly for the day after waking anxious and it clears my head of rumination by putting me in a calm state of mind and body to get to sleep and have a more restful sleep. It's a commitment to myself to set the tone for my day. It's programming my thoughts to go through it with acceptance, balance, and calm to respond to whatever happens rather than react. At the end of the day, it helps me to release any tension and relax my body and clears my mind to go to sleep.*"

Meditation has changed my life and it can yours. My friend Karen, a personal development follower like myself, recently drew my attention to ten-minute guided meditations for things like anxiety, sleep and more! Just Google "*Ten-Minute Meditations.*"

A case study on Meditation, Amanda. I posted some meditation on my EMOJI page, a Facebook group, and a client and friend, Amanda said this: *"Thank you for sharing. I am somewhat scared of meditation. I know it might sound strange, but I am scared I am doing it wrong. I listened to this in bed last night and fell asleep. I have had a lot of trouble falling asleep ever since all the trouble last year. Last year I was too scared to sleep at times. Maybe my brain and body remember. I will use it every night, I think. Thank you again."* (Rainbow, clapping hands and two love heart emojis.)

This was music to my ears. That I could help even one person to find their way to such a powerful yet simple strategy.

My coaching friend Harry is currently teaching meditation in a group he set up for people with cancer, or disease, a group for anyone looking for healing, harmony, being. *Overcoming Cancer*. He does a morning meditation almost every day and an "evening evolution." His commitment is extraordinary! Harry has also started a podcast called *Harry's Holistic Healing*. He has asked to interview me for an episode soon.

As mentioned previously, James teaches a very deep and powerful meditation as mentioned in the introduction. It is called *Human Re-engineering* or *Frequency Healing*. He has experienced major shifts.

Paul has a free e-book and teaches meditation regularly and has a huge following. People are looking for the inner calm we hear so much about. Movie stars advertise *transcendental Meditation.*

Courses are available all over the world. Buddhist temples and venues run free meditation events everywhere. It is part of their calling. My friend Karen and I recently attended one. The monk spoke Thai and there was a translator. The room was full of regular attendees. We received a lovely necklace with gold and a small crystal ball to remind us of part of the strategy, where we imagined the ball travelling inside our body. As mentioned, my daughter attended one with chants.

Many are like Amanda, scared to even start. Just start somewhere.

The Dalai Lama says that those who are too busy to meditate are those who need it most. I believe that a truer word has never been spoken. I would argue that those who say they don't need it, probably also need it the most!

I am so glad we are now teaching meditation in schools. Studies show just a few minutes a day can help with stress, sleep, and mental health. The best part is, it's free!

I did a five-day meditation course with Brett, from Perth, at Byron Bay. We shared our stories first to release some pain so we could benefit more from meditation. This can be vital. Because when the candle is lit, or we focus on the breath or the music is playing, our thoughts will often come back to the pain inside. If we can free some of that pain, we can focus more. See Brett's book *Awaken, Your Ultimate Spiritual Journey.* See *Resources*.

I stayed at a backpackers' "resort" opposite the beach. These are very cool places to stay, full of young people and they had the best café, full of old things. There was a timber and rope swing over at the beach, perfect for my inner child, little Sharon. I drove there in my friend's old black BMW as I loaned my car to Frank as his was getting fixed. Everything that week was way out of my comfort zone yet by the end of the week, I was ready to move to Byron Bay and work on my spiritual side. It was one of my best week's ever; a real adventure *all by myself* (said with a kid's voice.)

Meditation is like anything in life, it gets better with practice. Karen and I just tried a new kind at the beach where the presenter asked us to open our eyes and look around, which is a great idea to help us find peace and calm in our busy days. One day, a lady with a baby in a stroller, (pusher) set up her crystal sound bowl and we joined her for some healing vibes. I used to attend a monthly "Sound Bath" night on the Southside with my friend Tracey, where we all took yoga mats, cushions and blankets and listened to the vibrations of crystal bowls and other instruments, bells, and a rain stick. The hall was decorated with fairy lights. I found myself crying, feeling all sorts of energies and as Tracey predicted, my tummy was funny for days.

Yoga is designed to prepare the body for meditation.

I should point out here, that something I did not know until I learned meditation and yoga, is that yoga is designed to prepare the body for meditation. There are many great, simple meditation and breathing techniques such as box breathing where you imagine drawing a square, where you breath in for a count (let us say five seconds), imagining breathing up the side of the square, breathe out along the top of the square, then in again down the side then out along the bottom. You can also use your fingers to trace and breathe along them, called five-finger breathing. These techniques are wonderful for kids and beginners. Some may call them structured breaths.

I love a meditation called Yoga Nidra, where we focus on all body parts, this can take about twenty minutes and is very calming and effective. You can also find this easily online. Thanks, Pam, for teaching me Yoga Nidra.

Doubt nothing! Always keep an open mind. The stuff I have learned in the past 6 years is amazing! There is magic out there! You just need to be open minded and look! Seek and ye shall find.

Speaking of which... (Next heading...Manifestation)

For families: Meditation for kids is so easy, google to see what you all like. Try finding some for teens and teach them to do before bed or study. Use the box breathing and five finger breathing. If all else fails, just lead by example.

Manifestation.

There are many schools of thought on manifestation. Books like "*The Secret*" and follow up books started a huge trend towards something called manifestation. Manifestation can be believing the universe will provide for you. It can mean that if you visualise your dreams and believe in them, you can make them happen. It can mean certain people come into your life for a reason, that things happen for a reason. Some would believe it's a lot of nonsense. I was sceptical at first. You may be too.

Then, I started trying it. Doing vision boards and drawings of my dreams. Exercises with coaches where we imagine our dreams coming true. One coach, Tracey, at a meeting run by the amazing Beverley, who is in her seventies and on her journey, recently had us chatting with a partner. Asking them about their dream then imagining and role-playing meeting again in five or ten years. Asking them questions about how their dream turned out. This was amazingly powerful!

After reading the books, attending the courses, and trying it out, I concluded that manifestation is real, if we choose to act and make it happen!

An example or case study of manifestation, my house on the river.

So, for example, I have always wanted to live on the water. I recently sold my townhouse in a leafy suburb, Brisbane Southside and went looking around up here near the beach where I live with Frank. Homes at the beach are expensive. Homes on rivers up here on the Northside are often expensive and so far from Brisbane, my work, my family, and friends. I made a vision board with pictures of a home on the water. I said it will happen somehow. I wanted a property I could somehow redevelop to make my money work harder towards retirement. I looked at all the ways I could rustle up some extra money. I made enquiries about my superannuation. I set myself up for success. Then it happened. I took out a manageable loan.

I stumbled across an area just half an hour north of here, so about one hour north of the city. The area is called Beachmere and it is on the way to Bribie Island, which I love. I used to take my children there often. It is very old-world charm. Beachmere is on the Caboolture River. Frank and I went up and looked around at homes on the beach and river. The beach properties are out of my achievable price range. Then I stumbled across a property on two blocks of land with an ordinary house sitting over the two blocks.

I have moved two houses before, on trucks, so it is right up my alley! Bingo! The place is right on the river and has deep water access to Moreton Bay and Frank is a keen boatie and fisherman!

It did flood recently, and my tenant stayed on and moved upstairs while we renovated. I am applying for a grant to rebuild. I will shift the house across to one block, do a basic build underneath and hopefully manifest a way to build dual living for rental or a yoga studio. Frank would love a big shed with a mezzanine floor. The property has many fruit trees already and we want to build vegetable gardens. We want to work with a builder who specialises in sustainability. Frank and I have a You Tube channel and social media called *Sustainable Crusaders*. We promote sustainable living and relationships.

We will either sell the second block or find a way to keep it and maybe do another removal home. I would love to run yoga and fishing retreats. Ideas, ideas. Pick a dream, work out a way to make it happen. It is absolutely possible. Start with one small property where it costs no more than your rent. Allow for additional costs. Work your way up. The rental market is absolutely flooded. We need more owners and landlords. The stock market crashes, property prices fluctuate yet tend to improve or drop slightly then stabilise. At least in Australia. See *Resources* for a property guru or two to follow. Try Roy and Dympna.

Manifestation can mean meeting the right person at the right time. When you think, I wonder how Uncle Joe is going and he rings the next day. When you have such a connection with someone it feels "meant to be". When an event happens in your life, and it teaches you things. At maybe just the right time.

Life isn't happening to us; it's happening for us. Tony Robbins. *Life isn't happening to you; it's responding to you.* Rhonda Byrne, *The Secret.*

My current melanoma diagnosis.

I'm in a good place at the moment, both relationship wise and financially. I have a great support network. Cancer has come to teach me to slow down, focus on my health and do the things I've been wanting to do! Lessons being learned! Random event or not? Many people I have met over the past few years while on this amazing growth journey have been just the people I need to meet. Coincidence or not? I guess we believe what we choose to believe. I love the idea of manifestation.

*For families: Try a vision board or chart with kids, ask them what they would like to see happening for them, for the family and for the world. (See Appendix.) I have done them with my students, just by providing an A3 coloured chart or even larger, a bunch of magazines (available at charity stores, or ask around your friends and family) catalogues, travel magazines, and have a family workshop. You could do individual charts or a family chart. Sometimes one or more kids won't participate, that's ok, they have been invited. Always keep leading by example and do what you can.

Music.

Music is the language of the soul.

Pythagoras said, "Music is the language of the heart, the only language that enters the soul without having to pass through the filter of the brain first." And here we thought Pythagoras was a mathematician.

Do you ever notice how certain music makes you feel alive? Powerful? Sad? Music has a deep connection to the limbic system. This is the part of the brain involved in our behavioural and emotional responses. Music can trigger memories. Some songs have a powerful way of reminding us of a certain time or place, just like smells. It can create emotions.

I saw a video where an old man in an American nursing home had dementia and could remember very little, yet when they played old jazz music, he remembered the names of the artists and could explain all about them.

My favourite aunty loved her 1960's music. One of her favourites was "Tan Shoes and Pink Shoelaces." Her mate Jack and I were sitting with her towards the end of her cancer journey in her nursing home room. Aunty Jackie was on morphine and unconscious.

Jack and I were chatting and "including" Aunty Jackie in the conversation. We were drinking coke as it was her favourite drink.

I said to Jack, "Gosh this is a quiet party. Think I will go get a CD player and a CD." I found a CD with those types of tunes. Although Aunty Jackie had been unconscious for days and nonresponsive, she tapped her finger in time. At first, we didn't believe our eyes, yet it became obvious. It was an amazing moment, and a few tears were shed. So powerful!

Music can be used to uplift us. It can be used to sooth such as in meditation. Years ago, relaxation music became very popular. A rousing rendition of a powerful song like the 1812 Overture, or a favourite rock song can stir the soul. Try using a favourite old song when you need to cry and can't. It can be a huge release. Try lifting your spirits with some dance tracks in your living room when you're feeling down. Tony Robbins calls this "changing state."

For families: Use music in the home. Share each other's music. We used to play music videos every Sunday night for family (and friends) Barbecue night. Lisa started complaining about our music so we setup one of her "metal" bands and she was happy and surprised! Organise a family play list.

Morning ritual.

As mentioned in the Introduction and E for Evening Ritual, many famous people practise morning rituals. I have found these very powerful. The argument is how we start our day is how we intend to "operate" for the day, with purpose and calm. It's a bit like how I drink bone broth first up (apologies to vegans; maybe super greens) which lines my gut with healthy nutrients before coffee or tea. It's about what we put in first. (Or last in the case of evening or bedtime rituals.)

You can again "choose your own adventure", as explained in the Introduction about this EMOJI model. You can design whatever you choose for your rituals; it could be stretches, meditation (yoga is meant to prepare the mind and body for meditation), candles, incense, music, journaling, gratitudes, affirmations, whatever you like. As mentioned in the Introduction, designing your rituals can be a fun, creative process, you might even share with others: housemates, friends, partner, family.

The coach from Perth, Calvin, and his wife Ash, have a morning ritual where they ask each other what can I do for you today to support you or make your day better and similar questions. I love this. Some people do this in the morning and the evening. I just started a new ritual I saw on Facebook.

Upon waking:

1) State a gratitude

2) Set an intention for the day

3) Smile

4) Breathe, five deep breaths

5) Let go of yesterday's mistakes.

And I have added Calvin and Ash's

6) "What can I do to make your day better? To support you?"

Whatever you do, make it yours and adapt as you like along the way. Mine is walk the dog, Basil, a few stretches, and a meditation. Sometimes some journaling. At times, I do all of that, sometimes some of that, sometimes none depending on my schedule. Yet by doing it a few times a week, I feel great. Sometimes I add music, incense, and essential oil. Mindfulness on my walk. What can I smell, hear, see, touch and taste?

*For families: Try the ritual above and the mindfulness suggested with kids and teens. Involve the pets. Kids love this. Come up with family rituals.

Mastery.

Many coaching groups and coaches offer something called Self-Mastery. I did mine with Calvin, the coach from Perth and his team, the WILD team. I have since done coaching training and NLP (*neuro linguistic programming*) with them which is changing your thoughts and programming. I attended a three-day event in Brisbane initially and six months later I crewed for them and was suddenly blown away by how far I had come. Now a few years later, I know I knew so little. I then travelled to Bali to spend more time with the WILD team and became like a member of the family! I check in with them regularly and love seeing how many people they are helping. Transforming lives.

At the events and those of other coaches and coaching colleges, they sometimes have a whiteboard to write up people's "*limiting beliefs*". These are usually based on what we call the three universal fears: *not being loved, not being worthy (or good enough) and not belonging. Also: fear of trusting and surrendering, (aligns with not being worthy or good enough) abandonment and separation (not belonging). Gregg Braeden and others.* We also generally look at things like Tony Robbins' *six core needs* to see where our behaviour patterns are coming from and how we serve our needs with resourceful and unresourceful behaviours. We sometimes look at models like *The Wheel of Life* to see what areas our life needs support. Sometimes we look at models like below and above the line thinking and fixed and growth mindset. I am pleased to report we are doing a good deal of this work in schools now too and the coaching college from America that I am part of, *Adventures in Wisdom*, teaches a good deal of this to kids.

For families: Do a course with your kids and teens, give them self-help books to read. An American dad gave his teen books to read and paid him pocket money to read them. That boy is now a very wealthy person in the personal development world. Lead by example, share what you are trying. Do what you can.

Mission. (Or purpose)

It's amazing how new parts of the model leap out at me when I am putting this together. And some of them seem so obvious. Just today, while I am more than halfway through my first draft, I thought how obvious it would be to include *Mission*. And in our Emoji group of supporters, coaches, and people into personal development, we add strategies all the time. And even when I post something like I will right now, "Tell me about Mission", the team will add wonderful ideas.

Many people believe that we are all here for a purpose. I am certainly a big believer in this. I need a mission or purpose, always have. It helps me get out of bed. It helps me focus my activities. Right now, it is to get EMOJI written and shared. After that, Frank and I will be working on *Sustainable Crusaders* which EMOJI will be part of. We will be revamping and recreating.

We are excited for our lap of the country and spreading the word. When I met Frank, I was excited that he had a mission developing in his mind. He was lining up all his groceries wrapped in plastic and filming them. He was researching ways to reduce plastic and how much plastic people are finding at the beach and in the oceans.

It was funny because it had long been a passion of mine too. I had been recycling and growing veges and herbs. Buying second hand clothing and household items. Reducing, reusing, and recycling, *The Three Rs of Sustainability*. I had even sat with two mates one day, at my townhouse, my young friend Jay, and Colin (aka Gekko after Gordon Gekko, Wall Street), and we talked about creating a product to replace plastic bin liners, made of compostable biodegradable material, like corn starch "plastic". We came up with a groovy name which now escapes me. I recall thinking it was so clever, but no idea now and Jay can't remember. Gekko had an idea for greeting cards with a funny name and blunt messages. I can't disclose the name here in case he ever does it. I have since seen a similar concept and maybe one day I will help him develop the idea.

Have you ever had an idea? A mission, passion, or dream to change the world? Find a way to do it now! We are! Watch "Shark Tank" for people with a Mission.

I have had ideas all my life! Frank too. We are now combining our talents and building *Sustainable Crusaders*, with Facebook, Instagram and a You Tube channel called *Sustainable Crusaders AUS Adventures*. We started with *Crusaders Against Plastic*, then we have kept expanding and "pivoting" as they say in marketing, particularly during Covid to combine my EMOJI model and relationship and family coaching. Sustainable living! We are so excited to take this around the country in a year after my immunotherapy treatment for melanoma. And after we complete some home renovations on our two homes to rent or sell.

I once attended a conference for educational publishers and heard Bryce Courtney, the author of many best-selling books, deliver an after-dinner speech. I have told this story many times and even started writing a song which I must finish. He talked about how people lose their dreams. He talked about how they had dreams at twenty-one, like buying a red sports car and climbing a mountain. What happened to those dreams? As my coaching mate Harry says, "Don't die with your song in your heart."

I had many dreams as a kid and young adult. I married young, followed his dreams mostly and had my two kids late, in my mid to late thirties, after a few years teaching then educational publishing. I guess I didn't know what dreams to follow.

A few of the things I wanted to do involved an element of risk so had to wait. Sadly, we divorced about seven years ago and partly because we had such different goals and dreams. Don't get me wrong, by following his dreams I had some wonderful experiences. So did my kids.

Now it was time for my bucket list. Surfing, skateboarding, a tattoo for starters. Certainly not middle-aged mum material. Latin dancing, some travels, personal development, coaching studies. Being coached to reduce alcohol and heal some of my past. I am still ticking off my bucket list and will continue until they pop me in one of those boxes people can draw on.

Find or create your mission or purpose and follow your dreams! It will get you out of bed every day!
Sharon Chemello.

Just today on my very last day of writing the draft, I found a post by a coaching mate who does hypnosis, Jeremy, on my page I took over from another coach, Doug called *The Confidence Academy*. With Jeremy's permission, I thought this could be helpful:

#mindfulness #purpose

Which of these feels most like your purpose?

1. Caring for those who really need it.
2. Service to others.
3. Raise a family.
4. Do what you love every day.
5. Connection with people.
6. Helping others reach their potential.
7. Explore the world.
8. Express your inner truth.
9. Heal the planet.
10. Make a difference.
11. Love and be loved.

Love this list Jeremy, thank you. And to the universe for the synchronistic timing.

For families: Look at our mate Arlian, Plastic Free Boy, from Byron Bay, and what he has done for the environment and ocean with the help of his mum Karin, a film maker. Discuss with your kids and teens if they have a mission. Use vision boards. (See Appendix.) Use Jeremy's list above.

Motivation and Momentum.

In Steve's *I am Enough Academy* this month, we studied Momentum. It's not even something I've ever considered. Motivation yes. I'm aware that motivation can be about moving towards pleasure, or away from pain. Take alcohol reduction, smoking, or losing weight for example. Am I motivated towards being a healthier person or motivated by the pain it's causing me? Some say motivation versus inspiration.

Momentum includes motivation and inspiration. Steve gave us eight different aspects of momentum to consider. This is where education is so powerful. I love this stuff!

Magic, or Magik as many in the spiritual coaching world refer to it. There are even coaches I know who use Magik as their surname, or in their business name or marketing. My amazing friend Magdalena, who is a coach and Pilates instructor, reminded me recently of Roald Dahl's quote:

"And above all, watch with glittering eyes the whole world around you because the greatest secrets are always hidden in the most unlikely places. Those who don't believe in magic will never find it." Roald Dahl.

This quote is the last line from the last children's book written by Roald Dahl, *The Minpins.* Use Random Acts of Kindness, R.A.K.s like buying a coffee for a stranger (many coffee shops support this) or simply leaving a flower for someone.

Mentors, gurus and coaches.

*Find some people to follow. For you and your family or friends. (See *Resources.*)

Other M strategies.

Massage is hugely powerful for wellness. Nix says Movement for M. (Simple!) **What others could you add here in your notes?*

For families: Read "The Minpins", Roald Dahl, and focus on the quote about Magic. Discuss beliefs, create magic where you can. Have older children create magic for younger ones or drop a magical surprise gift to an elderly neighbour. Random acts of kindness. R.A.K.s. Leave a flower for sibling. Lead by example.

Please post more ideas in the group on Facebook any time to add to the model, we love it!

Notes for M.

☺
Chapter 8.

(Essential) Oils   Observe   Own your shizzle   Own your worth
Over the moon   Overcome challenges   Others
Opportunities

Let's look at some of these. This is not a complete list, it is some of my own from my training and reading and of the suggestions provided to me, by members of my group. There are more. Can you think of others? Leave a comment in the group and use the notes section at the end of the chapter.

(Essential) Oils.

I've always had an interest in aromatherapy, yet if you'd told me I'd be promoting essential oils and doing meditation a few years back, I'd have scoffed. Yet here I am. As part of my journey to wellness, I stumbled across many people doing essential oils. A now friend called Amanda, was showing oils at my local café, soon after I bought my townhouse. I went along and was amazed at what I learned about the benefits and the scents of the oils. Many oil people have particular oils they use with evidence-based choices for types of growing and harvesting, packaging and selling.

I bought a set of general *household essentials*. Later I bought a set of roll-on scents for emotions. I haven't looked back. Some I roll on neat, some I use in a diffuser. Some are beneficial for illness and prevention thereof. Some support the immune system. Some support emotions. One is amazing for arthritis. Amanda told me how even her sceptical dad was a convert when he saw how much it helped her mother's arthritis. My partner Frank has also had an amazing result. And myself too with an arthritic thumb. I have since met others doing oils. One of my friends, Lisa, has become my "go to". Another friend Valerie also works with oils. I must catch up with her soon!

I also include scents and incense here. Scented candles. Any aromatherapy.

Many people are having wonderful results in many areas of physical and mental health with CBD Oil.

For families: Try some essential oils with kids and teens. Follow Lisa, A Handle on Oils for more information, or Google. I gave my stepson Frankie a sage stick for "smudging" and cleansing the home and he lit it and waved it around the house for a half hour! Just be careful what you allow kids to use for fire safety. Gayle and Melissa even tell us to use with pets. Find out how.

Observe.

My good friend Karen, who I sit with every week at the beach, and we chat over all-things personal development and EMOJI, suggested *observe* as a component for EMOJI. We have both done many coaching programs including with Andrew, my greatest mentor and coach. One of the things that he and others teach is to come from curiosity. If you are being triggered by someone or something, come from curiosity to ask yourself questions as to why this is happening. Observe your behaviours and feelings. This can be a life changing strategy, especially for people with anger, anxiety, depression and so on.

When I was drinking and self-sabotaging, I would observe my own behaviour and ask myself the questions. "Why did you drink last night?" Usually when we "sit" with the feelings and work them out, something appears. Some say the answers are within us. I believe this to be true, and sometimes we need the help of a good coach to find them.

I was in a Telegram conversation with my coach Andrew about why I have trouble sitting and writing, when I enjoy it so much. Why I avoid and procrastinate. He asked me a bunch of questions about my fears. I brushed over, as I often do, and said "I don't like to sit still for long periods indoors." (Which is very true.) He said "No, you are brushing over the truth. What are you afraid of? You said there was a level of fear."

Yes, it's the imposter syndrome where we feel we are not good enough. Who am I to think I know enough to write a book on personal development? This can be called facing the shadow. I am an imposter. I'm a two-bit, weekend warrior coach who thinks she is good enough to write the book.

Bingo!

*Feel it, face it, sit with it. Deal with it. Heal it. * Find your shadows and face them for healing. Follow Andrew Pearce for more on this work.*

Observe your behaviour, rather than coming from judgement. Tapping is helpful here. (See EFT). When I was drinking, I would "beat myself up". Then I learned how to come from curiosity and observation and ask myself the questions and without judgment, tap on the words "Did a silly thing, we all do silly things, I love and respect myself anyway". Thank you, Marie, for that one.

You can observe others too. Why does my partner sometimes over supervise me in the kitchen? Why did my friend or family member snap at me when I said …? One of the greatest things I've learned is to come from love not fear. But even just to observe can be so helpful! The more you learn about human behaviour, the more you can do this.

There are coaches who can teach you so much more about human behaviour. There are well known and widely accepted personality profiles to help you identify your traits and needs. Even something as simple as *The Five Love Languages* by Gary Chapman can help you identify what love languages speak to you or any loved one including your kids or a partner.

There is a reason why teenagers (more often girls) used to do magazine quizzes (and now people do online quizzes) to find out more about themselves or a potential partner. There are reasons people enjoy star signs. Many workplaces use personality profiling in job interviews, or training. The coaching college where I have studied, uses a profiling tool that identifies what kind of creator/worker you might be. I have done personality profiles at many self-mastery events. In some circles I am a goal driven shark/playful dolphin. In other circles I am a manifester/generator.

Observing can be a really useful tool to teach children. I even have a friend, Alan, who teaches facial profiling, where certain facial features can suggest certain personality traits. This can be used to help your children, or your business.

For families: Gary Chapman's *The Five love languages of Children. Corey's book The Little Book of BIG Emotions. Discuss feelings and observe behaviour. Teach kids and teens to be curious about their behaviour and others'. Use movies for discussion points. Watch "The Social Dilemma", a great documentary, to teach kids and teens about social media and its effects on us.*

Own your shizzle.

This is the big one! How much time do you have? Grab a cuppa and sit back for this one.

In coaching we often start with a model called "*above and below the line thinking*". If you Google this model, there are many versions you could print out for your refrigerator or noticeboard or draw on your whiteboard. It's one of the first models I offer clients.

Here's a simple version:

Above the line:
Ownership
Accountability — Can we explore that more so I can better understand?
Responsibility

Below the line:
Blame
Excuses — Well, that's because of XYZ..
Denial

I have taught this to children who are learning to take responsibility for their actions.

*Also Google "Fixed and Growth Mindset".

Teacher (me): "He swore at you because you hit him, do you understand that?"

Johnny: "Yes but he said the F word!"

Me: "I understand but wasn't that after you hit him?"

Johnny: "Yeah but he said I was stupid!"

Me: "Could you walk away? Use your words? All the things we have talked about?"

Johnny: "Yeah but aren't you gonna go mad at him for swearing at me?"

If I had a dollar for every one of these conversations, I would be rich! You may even know adults who operate at this level.

I even had a mother approach me in my spare time at the swimming pool, after school, while my children had their swimming lessons, to ask me why I had put her son out of the soccer game. I explained that her son was the (self-appointed) captain and was bullying his players. Calling them hopeless and yelling at them. I gave him two warnings and said unless he could encourage his players with language like "good try" and "better luck next time", he would need to sit out for five minutes. The mother said, "Well he is a very good player." I replied, "Well I feel that he needs to learn to be a good captain and a good captain encourages his team." She started to say more, so I interrupted with "I'm sorry, I'm here on my own time. And it's my job to teach the children." I had another mother talk to me about an incident with her daughter where her daughter and four other girls were, I feel, "bullying" another child. She said, "You don't know the history." I even had a teacher tell me she was sick of hearing the word "bullying" when I told her about a very clear case in her class.

I have certainly recognised myself as a helicopter parent. Years ago when it was pointed out to me and even lately by my adult children. We try to protect our kids, it's a control mechanism. They are better off when we teach them resilience. Thanks, Basia, school admin officer, for telling me to not bring my daughter's sports shoes to school anymore, she needs to learn to remember them.

Helicopter parents are those who hover around, taking teachers and bosses to task, instead of letting their kids learn the hard way, learning resilience. This is a whole other book!

Don't get me wrong, I've done it myself. Instead of letting my kids own their behaviour and instead of letting teachers, bosses, coaches, and friends treat my kids their way. The absolute best things we can teach kids are resilience by trial and error and how to cope with disappointment. Otherwise, we are pandering to them. This in turn can create a lack of resilience, a lack of ownership and even a level of narcissism. Perfectionism can be a curse and create anxiety. These are all my opinions. Another book perhaps.

When I teach Visual Arts, all my students are taught to say, "There are no mistakes in Art." Otherwise the same child will toss out up to ten sheets of quality paper. I have seen it many times. They will use an eraser over and over. (Some teachers don't even allow erasers.) They will tear up their work. At the end of the lesson, they will have nothing done. Leonardo da Vinci had thousands of sketches as did Vincent Van Gogh.

Ownership of our "behaviours" is vital. I remember someone saying "You can't make kids apologise. They need to feel it or it's not genuine, what's the point?" Ok, where do you want me to start? From the time they are babies, we ask them to say, "Thank you" and some even accept "Ta" as a substitute. "Sorry" is just as important, in my opinion. This is why courts are now implementing victim statements and reconciliation. This is how we learn how our behaviour affects others.

When we have an altercation in the classroom, I do my best as a teacher to come from a space of non-judgment. I often ask the "perpetrator" to look at the victim and see how they are feeling. I sometimes ask the victim to say how they are feeling. This is one of the ways we can teach emotional intelligence. I might ask the perpetrator "Do you understand you have hurt her feelings?" These conversations can be so vital. If possible, other kids can be involved so we all learn together. Sometimes the conversations need to be had after class.

On addictive behaviours and "owning your shizzle".
Russell Brand has an amazing book on addiction. He has set up a system similar to the Alcoholics Anonymous (AA) twelve step system. I won't go into it here, but I absolutely love it. It's rather hard hitting. Basically, it goes something like this: *"Have you f*#ked up? How have you f*#ked up? How could you unf*#k yourself and do you need help?"*

He also tells how exercise, meditation and support through connection helped him. I love this model so much; I've even thought of asking Russell if I could run workshops for him. One day I might just send that message. My crazy creative mind even had me imagining doing workshops dressed as Russell, complete with black hair and an English accent. These are the ideas that wake me at 3am. But I deal with them by using the sleep program mentioned in Energy and Resources.

There are many types of addiction: Substance addictions, including alcohol, drugs, and food. Behavioural addictions which might include things like self-sabotaging behaviours such as staying up late, internet addiction, gaming, social media, porn, even gossiping, drama cycle and anger. Impulse addictions such as buying things, gambling, and sex. Go to Tom for alcohol and Catherine for porn. See the *Resources* at the end of the book.

Addictions can be due to emotional triggers, the search for stimulation or pleasure, comfort, self-punishment, or self-harm, rebellion, wanting to change the way we feel and so much more. Addictions can be managed with the right help and lack of judgment can help. I know coaches who deal with most forms of addiction. I have beaten an alcohol addiction myself with the help of an amazing Australian coach, Tom. As I write this book, I am working with a more spiritual coach, Andrew, facing shadows from my past (patterns of behaviour that are self-sabotaging) to "unlearn" them.

A popular post I saw on social media recently was:

"Sometimes I wake up and have to remind myself: There is nothing wrong with me. I have patterns to unlearn, new behaviours to embody and wounds to heal. But there is nothing wrong with the core of me and who I am. I am unlearning generations of harm and remembering love. It takes time." (Source unknown.)

Many coaches will say *"We aren't broken, we don't need fixing."* However, I believe at some stage we need to own our stuff and maybe even make amends. We need to learn to apologise when we have hurt people. Or be prepared to be very lonely. Everyone makes mistakes. It's about owning them and yes, maybe "fixing" them in some way.

A favourite book of mine is one from many years ago called "*All I Really Need to Know I Learned in Kindergarten.*" By Robert Fulghum. My favourite American neighbour Chuck gave it to me when I was young, before I became a mum.

Here are the rules:

"These are the things I learned (in kindergarten):

1. Share everything.
2. Play fair.
3. Don't hit people.
4. Put things back where you found them.
5. CLEAN UP YOUR OWN MESS.
6. Don't take things that aren't yours.
7. Say you're SORRY when you HURT somebody.
8. Wash your hands before you eat.
9. Flush.
10. Warm cookies and cold milk are good for you.
11. Live a balanced life - learn some and drink some and draw some and paint some and sing and dance and play and work every day some.
12. Take a nap every afternoon.
13. When you go out into the world, watch out for traffic, hold hands, and stick together.

14. Be aware of wonder. Remember the little seed in the Styrofoam cup: The roots go down and the plant goes up and nobody really knows how or why, but we are all like that.
15. Goldfish and hamster and white mice and even the little seed in the Styrofoam cup - they all die. So do we.
16. And then remember the Dick-and-Jane books and the first word you learned - the biggest word of all - LOOK." *Robert Fulghum, All I Really Need to Know I Learned in Kindergarten*.

I believe that if we all followed a simple list of rules like this, the world could be a better place. Maybe I will contact Robert Fulghum if he is still alive (Postscript, he is!) and see what we could do with this list? It's so pertinent, especially in these times of social media and family breakdown, the first seven are vital for owning your shizzle. After that, the rest are about creating a better life, full of emoji, joy, peace, and love.

There was a list of manners displayed in schools many years ago. An old friend and college lecturer Graham, gave me a copy. It was a chart that hung in every classroom in Queensland and was based on a chart from the UK in 1889 and was used from 1898.

It was considered part of the systemic teaching of conduct and manners.

"The rules covered personal conduct at home, at school, at play, in the street, at the table and general courtesy. School rules emphasised that children should respect teachers, other students and school property. Cheating, dishonesty and cowardice were discouraged at school and play." (Queensland Department of Education: History Topics.) * Google and print out for the family for fun. Or you can order online.

Various school inspectors reported improvement in behaviour, or not. I guess behaviour is a very subjective thing. I'm sure many of the older generation would bemoan how the manners and behaviour have "gone out the window" and they often suggest ways to improve them, often with returns to past strategies like corporal punishment. This is a whole other debate and I once again refer to Lillian's work on The Nurtured Heart Approach. (See Resources.)

Ho'oponopono is own your shizzle.
(See also forgiveness under Inner work.)

There is a beautiful procedure called Ho'oponopono, practiced in the islands. I love this method and would like to train to become a practitioner.

Ho'oponopono is a traditional Hawaiian practice of reconciliation and forgiveness. The Hawaiian word translates into English simply as correction, with the synonyms manage or supervise. Similar forgiveness practices are performed on islands throughout the South Pacific, including Hawaii, Samoa, Tahiti and New Zealand.

The practice of Ho'oponopono will do just that and the good news is that you can do it in just four easy steps.

What are the 4 phrases of Ho'oponopono?

- Step 1: Repentance – JUST SAY: I'M SORRY. ...
- Step 2: Ask Forgiveness – SAY: PLEASE FORGIVE ME. ...
- Step 3: Gratitude – SAY: THANK YOU. ...
- Step 4: Love – SAY: I LOVE YOU. (*Wikipedia*)

Ho'oponopono is "owning your shizzle" in a wonderful creative and prayerful way. Isn't it wonderful how we can learn from other cultures? Makes me wonder what else is out there to learn from.

For example, **Kintsugi.** Kintsugi is a Japanese philosophy and craft where they take a broken item of china or ceramics and mend it with gold leaf in the cracks - a metaphor for embracing your flaws and imperfections. That something broken becomes a thing of beauty and worth. What a wonderful idea. This refers to my comments in the *Introduction* that we are not "broken" and that in fact, the cracks or faults are a golden part of us. "You won't realize your full potential until you go through the tough times," Kumai says. Japanese modern-day philosopher.

What does Kintsugi teach us about life? Kintsugi teaches you that your broken pieces make you stronger and better than ever before. When you think you are broken, you can pick up the pieces, put them back together, and learn to embrace the cracks. Kintsugi teaches you that your broken pieces make you stronger and better than ever before. (Wikipedia)

I reckon Kintsugi tells us it's ok to own your shizzle, it's part of you! My amazing coaching friend Heather, who passed away last year, talked about being *Flawesome,* combining the word awesome and flaws.

 *For families: Teach these models, especially above and below the line, or Google fixed and growth mindset. Discuss openly with kids.

Own your worth. (self-love)

I'm adding this one at the last minute, like many strategies. For weeks, I've been writing notes in my car (when stationary) and at home. I think the model is finished (knowing it is of course infinite) then I hear something, or someone gives me another strategy to add. Some of them are a case of "I can't believe I didn't have that one." And of course, it's been challenging and fun to fit all the strategies in the letters of EMOJI.

Own your worth is so important to combat the limiting beliefs or universal fears of "*I'm not good enough, I'm not worthy, I'm not loved, I don't belong.*" Way back, I did a couple of courses on Self Love with Andrew and also Aime Maire.

No matter what you grew up with, no matter what has happened to you in relationships, you can find your worth and self-love. It takes time and healing work. It's a bit like the gratitudes; it takes more than positive affirmations on post it notes on the bathroom mirror.

There are many simple strategies you can try. Affirmations, Tapping (See EFT), coaching, or seeing a counsellor or psychologist, reading, and doing courses on this topic, trying new things such as dating yourself, stepping outside your comfort zone to try activities that might bring fear, to increase your self-confidence. Look at *The Wheel of Life Model* and see where you can improve aspects of your life. Do things that make you proud of yourself. And celebrate each win.

Lillian calls it similar to this, focussing on strengths, Inner Wealth, see I for Inner Wealth.

For families: Use the Resources section to find coaches who teach all of this. Build your kids and teens inner wealth. And your own.

Other O strategies.

Overcoming Challenges, much of this book can help with this. This would lead to resilience as a strategy. Something we can teach children. Stephanie runs a group called *Let's Raise Emotionally Intelligent Kids*.

Opportunities, see Manifestation.

Outside. The best place for feeling alive, getting vibes from nature!

For families: See Resources for coaches. Get the family outside. Bocce is a quick easy outdoor challenge. Any lawn games. Or at the beach or park. Go for family outings. Make it a regular thing so teens complain less, allow kids to bring a friend if possible.

***Please post more ideas in the group on Facebook any time to add to the model, we love it!*

Notes for O.

Chapter 9.
J

Journaling (The Three J's) – Jealousy, Judgement, Justification
Journey   Joy   Jaunts   Just be   Jovial   Jokes
Join in   Jigsaws   Justice

Let's look at some of these. This is not a complete list, it is some of my own from my training and reading and of the suggestions provided to me, by members of my group. There are more. Can you think of others? Leave a comment in the group and use the notes section at the end of the chapter.

Journaling

Journaling can be a useful strategy for change. When I was growing up, most girls had a diary. Some had locks on them. Now journaling is recommended by many coaches and authorities. As this is written, a top psychologist in Canada is recommending an online program he sells about writing your story. I just printed out another *writing your story* piece I saw on Facebook that I liked. Once you get "into" personal development, all kinds of things will pop up for you. Many of them free materials and courses.

Journaling can be part of your daily rituals, morning, or evening, and can include affirmations or gratitudes. It can include things that are going well for you and things you'd like to improve. There is a great deal of evidence that the brain link between the mind and the hand can be very powerful. I am in a group called *The Happiness Co* with Julian Pace and his team, where we posted gratitudes every day. Some of my friends still do this. Somewhere along my journey, someone taught me to do five gratitudes a day. I'm not sure who it was yet I like this method.

What am I grateful for?
What am I happy about?
What am I excited for?
What am I proud of?
What am I committed to?

When I was at my lowest point, I would write these every day. Sometimes I felt like I had no answer. I would write about what was happening which helped to release pain and find gratitude.

Disclaimer: Some will say we can't force gratitudes or affirmations. I agree. I have found much more gratitude by healing my trauma and letting go of the past! Then I have a general peace and calm that naturally creates gratitude.

For families: Get everyone a journal, go to Officeworks or the cheap shop to let them choose. Discuss gratitudes and what else they might contain and lead by example.

The three J's: Jealousy, judgement, and justification.

I had some coaching before I left home, with Jennifer, a teacher who was coaching in her spare time and I don't even recall how I found her. I think I saw something on a community notice board. I think she was studying with a group who I have learned more about and some of my friends have trained with.

The funny part is, I was teaching at a Catholic school set up by the Josephite nuns, or Sisters of St Joseph, led by our first Saint in Australia, Blessed Mary McKillop, whose garments had an emblem of 3 J's. (For Jesus, Joseph and John the Baptist who baptised Jesus in a river.) Nothing at all to do with the other, but interesting to me. Maybe an obscure link? My creative mind can find one for sure!

Jenni taught me about the 3 J's and how they are something to be aware of in our everyday lives. She also offered me a "rebirth" which sounded very woo woo but was actually very powerful. Anyway, that's a story for another time. But it is an example of the many and wide-ranging strategies for wellness out there.

I became conscious of how often I judge, justify and am jealous. Wow! Even on social media, at the shops, watching television, at work, when I meet new people. As these can be unresourceful strategies in life, if they don't serve us, it's great to come from curiosity (O for Observe, thanks Karen) and ask why we do this each time and attempt to lift our game or raise our vibration as they say. ("*On raising your vibration*" in the Introduction pages)

For families: Discuss and observe times when we all use these 3 Js. Lead by example. "Correct" yourself and tell your kids.

Journey

My young coaching friend Harry mentioned journey recently and I said, "That's going straight to EMOJI!" We are all on a journey in our lives. Who we travel with and where we go is up to us and maybe the universe? There is a lovely meme on Facebook that talks about our train of life. People come on our train; people get off. Some stay with us a short time, some with us a long time. There are many different versions, but it goes something like this.

"Life is like a train journey, with its stations, with changes of routes and with accidents. When we are born, we meet our parents, and we believe they will always travel with us. However, at some station, our parents step down from the train, leaving us on this journey alone. As time goes by, other people will board the train and they will be important: siblings, friends, children, and partners. Many will step down and leave a permanent hole. Others will go unnoticed, and we won't even realise they left their seats, which is very sad when you think about it. This train ride will be full of joy, sorrow, fantasy, expectations, hellos, goodbyes, and farewells. Success means having a good relationship with all the passengers, requiring that we give our best. The mystery to everyone is: we do not know at which station we will step down. So, we must live our best way: love, forgive and give the best of who we are. This is important because when the time comes to step down and leave our seat empty, we should leave behind beautiful memories for those who will continue to travel on the train of our life. I wish you a joyful journey on the train of your life. Reap success and give lots of love. More importantly, give

thanks for the journey. Thank you for being part of my journey."

Author unknown, quoted by many. Various versions.

Or as Harry says*: "Don't die with your song in your heart."* A well-known expression.

I mentioned the author Bryce Courtney, in M for mission or purpose and how he argued that we must live our dreams. Buy your sports car, climb that mountain.

In the coaching industry, we talk about the healing journey, or the journey to self. Sometimes it's even called *"The Hero's Journey"*. You might go on a wellness journey and in fact when I posted this question in the Emoji group and typed in "journey" to find a GIF, the wellness journey came up.

One coaching friend, Bernie, sent me a quote on New Year's Eve: "*Life is not about finding oneself, but creating yourself.*" I love this quote as I am living proof that I have become the person I've wanted to be in just a few short years.

My friend, Farmer Gregie from Beaudesert in Queensland, is on a journey through Mexico and Southeast Asia as we speak, or as this is written in August 2022. This is a huge journey for him, first time outside his country town and a growth and healing journey. *Postscript, he is home now and telling his story.*

When Frank and I go around Australia next year, preaching sustainability, this will be a massive journey.

Your journey can be anything you want it to be. You are the creator of your dreams. A much-quoted example of this is that Colonel Sanders was sixty-five when he released his recipe for Kentucky Fried Chicken. If you think you have nothing special to offer, think again. I wanted to be an author and here I am at almost sixty, finally writing my book. I wanted to study psychology and now I am, through coaching studies. I wanted to climb a mountain, I did that a few years ago with two girlfriends in New Zealand. I might do another. I dreamed of a place on the water, and last year, I was able to buy a place. I have worked hard to do that, renovating many homes with my ex-partner. Saving money. Then since separation, I have built up my own wealth to be able to do this.

There is a father and son coaching team in the USA where the father offered the boy twenty dollars to read a self-help book, then another and another. The boy became very knowledgeable on coaching models and personal development and became a coach himself. They are, I'm sure, making plenty of money, and more importantly, helping so many people.

I wanted to learn to surf and skateboard, so I did at age fifty-three. I've jumped out of a plane. I will do a balloon ride. I have sat in a racing car on the track, (Thanks Gekko), ridden motor bikes and I want to learn to sail and will most likely do that. There are places I would like to visit. I will do all I can. I want to teach yoga and I will, and make artwork for people, I have and will again. I have been a DJ and a model. I have played guitar and sung on stage. I have been on TV.

I grew up in a regular working-class family in the Air force. My mum and dad were regular people, although they both had high intelligence, gifts, and talents. Dad had many dreams but sadly couldn't fulfil many. Mum has been able to fulfil quite a few. We had no more opportunity than anyone else.

I just posted the question in my group and Coach Terri says: *Journey of life, transformation, discovery, travel for pleasure. Learning, evolving, growing, change.*

Coach Emma W says: *Journey is many, many paths. It doesn't matter which path you choose, ultimately you will end up at the same destination but will experience different scenery.*

Coach Donna-Lee says: *The Journey is the ultimate destination. It's the path you take that you learn your lessons, celebrate your milestones, and ultimately living it this very moment.*

You can be and do anything you want if you put your mind to it and believe in yourself. If you have "limiting beliefs", please see a coach.

*For families: Discuss and plan journeys together. Physical journeys and mental/ spiritual journeys. Lead by example. My young adult daughter, Lisa and I just went on a four-wheel drive camping weekend for women. One day we hope to do a walk in New Zealand together. Frank and I are off to Uluru in three weeks to see my teaching friend Cae. We are taking time off work. But life is short. Use your journal to plan and take action on your mental health and spiritual journey using EMOJI.

Joy! The chicken and the egg.

*Joy is all around us, but we must search for it. And create it. Go for a mindfulness walk. When we have anxiety and depression, joy feels hard to find.

All the strategies in this book will help you to create more joy.

*For families: Start with small things and build joy over time, what used to make you laugh? What used to give you gratitude? Or your family member or friend? Help them to find theirs! Watch Man Vs. Bee, Rowan Atkinson, Netflix. Stand up comedy of your choice. Play a family game. Or with a friend. Lay on the grass and look at clouds! Last night Frank and I saw a witch on a broomstick on a moonlit night.

Other J strategies.

"Just be" could be a whole book! Staying in the moment. Not expecting any particular outcomes or worrying about the past or future. This can be helped with meditation and breathwork strategies to let go such as facing shadows (*Andrew Pearce for this work*). *Read Eckhart Tolle.*

Jokes. There are many laughter coaches. They say *laughter is the best medicine*. If you feel that laughter would help you, hit me up for coaches in this area. Practise using humour every day, it's vital. Create humour, enjoy humour!

For families: Use mediation, mindfulness and breathwork with family. Discuss memes about being in the moment. Watch comedies together. Crack Dad jokes. Free your inner child. Show your kids.

* Please post more ideas in the group on Facebook any time to add to the model, we love it!

Notes on J

☺
Chapter 10.
I

The I letter has many strategies.

Ice Man   Inner Health   Inner Child   Inner Work   Inspire
Inner Peace and Calm   Interaction   Influence   Introspective
Interests   Independence   Ideas   Ideals   Impact

Let's look at some of these. This is not a complete list, it is some of my own from my training and reading and of the suggestions provided to me, by members of my group. There are more. Can you think of others? Leave a comment in the group and use the notes section at the end of the chapter.

Ice Man.

The first one is pretty wild: Ice man, Wim Hof. You may have heard about him. He has climbed mountains and walked in freezing and sweltering temperatures, using the power of the mind over the body. He has ice baths. He teaches breathwork. He teaches us that the mind is capable of anything! At least more than we think we are capable of. I recall an Australian Journalist, Todd Samson, who did a show about the mind and its power, and he went from holding his breath for a minute under water to many minutes.

In some cultures, people can go away and will themselves to die. Some people can live unexpectedly, by using the power of the mind.

We are way more powerful than we give ourselves credit for. Maybe this part should be called Inner Power!

I am not keen on ice baths or walking and climbing areas unprepared, without a great deal of training, but I have used cold showers and cold swims for helping to "shock" anxiety. By taking a cold shower or having a cold swim, we can "burn up" the adrenaline, cortisol and chemicals that are causing anxiety. I once did a cold swim in the family swimming pool for a challenge my son wanted to film, called "*Doing it for the vine.*" It was May in Brisbane and getting quite cold. My son's friend Jack said, "You won't do it", which of course spurred me on. We posted the video on Facebook with my son shouting, "for the Vine!" and me diving in then shuddering loudly at the cold. I felt so good, and I was proud of myself for taking on a challenge and being a cool mum. The pride of doing something outside our comfort zone can be very powerful. I heard one coach say recently that if he has a cold shower, everything else in his day looks easier.

You may hear your inner child saying, "I did it!"

Breathwork has been a part of Yoga and meditation for centuries. Wim Hof has taught his own methods and there are many practitioners all over the world. Some people get amazing results from breathwork, and I have certainly found it helpful. My coaching mate Harry is currently teaching "structured breaths" in meditation. My coaching mate Steve teaches simplistic breathwork. I want to do more training soon with Nicholas.

Sometimes when I'm doing a video for EMOJI, I will lose track of the "I" strategies and say, "Inner everything." Because *inner* is where everything happens! Let's go through all the *inners*!

*For families: Try cold showers, baths, swims. Lead by example. Google for breathwork and try strategies with kids and teens.

Inner child.

Inner child work is some of the most powerful work we can do. I can imagine Yoda saying, "The inner child is powerful in this one."

It is well known among academics, teachers, psychologists, coaches, counsellors, and psychiatrists that the formative years are ages zero to seven. You may sometimes hear it linked with the term *socialisation* and others which mean how we learn and what shapes us. The theories tell us, that how we are treated and what happens when we are small, shapes us into who we become. Some call this *imprinting*.

A simple example might be that our mother is always worrying about money or paying bills, so we grow up with a "*limiting belief*" about money and we grow up believing money can be a problem. We can work on this as an adult, with practitioners who know about this theory. Hypnosis can be very powerful here, as well as *Timeline Therapy* and *Neuro Linguistic Programming* (NLP).

I remember when I first started learning about the power of the inner child and taking care of her. I put pictures of my five and seven-year-old self on my pin board to support her, even my twelve-year-old which was a massive transition time for me in many ways. I had just moved to a new school, was starting high school, had my first real boyfriend, who was my soulmate and absolute love, first period and measles. I was a bridesmaid for my aunty in Queensland, my class went to Canberra, it was all happening.

I was tall and awkward, a tom boy, and I felt like I didn't fit in. I had an awkward relationship with my dad who drank and teased me. Mum was stressed, doing her best and my siblings faced challenges as special needs kids. I knew I was special, intuitive, and empathic. I knew I was meant for something else. I loved challenges riding my bike, building cubbies in the bush, and even riding a motor bike I had won from the circus while I was go karting there every day, beating the boys.

I have used the inner child strategy with many clients and asked them to put up photos and talk to that child and support them, asking them what they need. Often, we can identify our pain and hurt and find people to help us heal. I had a hugely powerful session with a healing coach called Yvonne, where we talked about what happened with my dad many years ago and what would my five-year-old say to him. She used coaching strategies and Reiki. I am eternally grateful to Yvonne.

We can use inner child to re-parent ourselves, to change outcomes. This can be massively powerful work and needs to be done carefully, in capable, trained hands. Read reviews and ask around.

Inner child work can be for something we have let go

or squashed or pushed down. One thing I enjoy with my partner Frank is a huge sense of inner child. We poke out our tongues and we say the line from the M and M commercial, "You get in the bowl" often. We tease and pull hair. Some people have lost this ability to play. Coach Harry and I talk about it often.

Try saying "na na na na na" at the top of your lungs. See how good that feels?

I had a coaching friend Claire, set up a group about the inner child, called *The Inner Child Project* on Facebook, but she let it go as she found a different job. I just stopped my writing to send her a message. The wonderful thing about writing this book is realising how many people have influenced me along the way. *Postscript, Claire is off Facebook, but you can still find the project.*

A friend, Ross on Kangaroo Island once said:" We take a small piece of everyone we meet." I love this.

When I do my live videos about the EMOJI model, I almost always say "Jump in puddles and lay on the grass and look at clouds, see if you can find the Easter Bunny or a unicorn." Watch small children and see what they do, you will learn so much, they are so full of life and joy! Lisa and I still poke each other and say "Get to Preschool" sometimes. When she was little and dragging her feet on the way to preschool, on the walking track near our house, I would poke her with a stick or umbrella and say, "Get to Preschool." It was a fun game we played.

My son Marco once gave me a large sign he had bought and he carried it home from the shops, walking about a half kilometre, for Mother's Day or my birthday. Strangely, it was when I was going through a hard time at home. Marco is most certainly an empath. Both my kids are. I'm lucky. Empathy can be nurtured, or taught, too. The sign said: *"Stop waiting for the rain to pass, learn to dance in the rain."*

Then Lisa gave me a small plaque which sits by my bed:

"Sing like no one's listening, dance like no one's watching, love like you've never been hurt and live each day as if it were your last." I love this quote.

*Learn to embrace your inner child; set them free!

Find or create an inner child bucket list and tick it off!

When I used to run some cabins in the bush at Stanthorpe, in the Granite Belt near the New South Wales border, an elevated and cold place, known as bushranger country, a way that I marketed them was to list activities for kids and teens. There were challenges, from a road trip quiz to things to do around the cabins and surrounding area. This earned me an offer to be on the local tourism board as not many people were promoting to families and considering children, most were focusing on couples or groups doing wine tours. Yet there were rocks and trees to climb, bushwalks, yabby catching, dams with frogs, fires to build and even a bushranger hideout. I made lists suitable for younger kids and even teenagers with a prize of a bandana from Canteen, a charity for kids dealing with cancer. For the younger ones, small stuffed Aussie animals. The parents loved the activities and kids asked to come back to our cabins. The parents told me that they wanted to complete the list too. I said, "Why not?"

Embrace and free your inner child, try one new thing a day. You may need to step outside your comfort zone. Try starting with hugging or climbing a tree.

Send me a message, let me know how you go, I will be elated. Or better still, post your experience in our EMOJI group, complete with a photograph. I dare ya! I will probably be doing more on Instagram soon for the younger ones and maybe even a splash of Tik Tok.

The most important part of inner child is however, healing the inner child. You may notice when you have a fight with someone, you are saying things that may be coming from your hurt inner child. When you say something like "You're always nagging at me" what you really mean is "I don't like this. I feel hurt when you tell me I'm not good enough." This is acknowledging your inner child.

This is an effective way to communicate.

The three universal fears, as mentioned in the introduction, according to Gregg Braden and others, are:

I'm not worthy or good enough

I'm not loved

I don't belong.

Also: fear of trusting and surrendering, (aligns with not being worthy or good enough) abandonment and separation (not belonging).

If we get curious or O for Observe our feelings, we can often see these feelings playing out and so often they are inner child feelings. As mentioned, a good practitioner can help you release these feelings. Next year I will be coaching one on one and teaching group programs to accompany the book. You can always find me on Facebook. Message me any time. Contact details are in the back of the book.

For families: Jump in puddles, lay on the grass, and watch clouds, have a cherry spitting competition, be a fun parent, partner, or sibling. Enjoy life! Create fun times.

Inner work.

Doing the *inner work* is a well-used coaching term. My coaching friend and mentor Steve Barker even has a podcast of this name.

Before I started this journey of personal development, I had no idea what I needed to learn. I had read a few books such as "*Women Who Do Too Much*, "Don't *Sweat the Small Stuff*" and many others such as one on calm and one on mindfulness. I was always interested. I visited counsellors, doctors, a psychiatrist when I went in for a stay at the post-natal ward in a psychiatric hospital, I'd seen physio, acupuncturist, chiropractor, doctors who practice structural mechanics, a naturopath, a psychic and more! I'd tried Yoga, meditation, mindfulness studies, the gym, swimming, martial arts and Tai Chi, Judo, massage, and any strategy I found out about through Facebook or elsewhere.

Sadly, during an argument, someone close to me snapped "You're always looking for answers!" I didn't know where to start. Firstly, yes, I was. Because I knew they were out there. I knew there were answers to the riddle of mental health and wellness. I knew that people who go off on a lengthy retreat and find peace and calm with the monks who were onto something. I would still like to do this. In fairness to this person, I was pretty messed up and they were frustrated. I need to do this work.

I went on to say that this is why people study self-help or personal development, attend church, study philosophy, psychology, go off on retreats, go live in hippy communes. To find the inner peace they know is attainable.

I'm still on my journey, but I have found so many answers. Earlier I mentioned *The Scale of Consciousness, David Hawkins*. I may never reach enlightenment although I can honestly tell you when you meditate regularly, you will have moments of this. I have come from lower-level emotions such as fear, anger, guilt and shame up through moderate emotions such as acceptance to peace, love, and joy. I'm so grateful for this journey and so pleased to be teaching it to others.

Writing this book has been hard work. I'm not good at sitting still for long, I sometimes am afraid of

Imposter Syndrome (what would *she* know?) and limiting beliefs of I'm not worthy, or the book might flop! In other words, the universal fears, not good enough, not loved and don't belong. Then I have a chat with my support crew and get cracking again! I know this stuff works. If "higher level" coaches who know more than me, have deeper learnings, I am not too concerned! I have massive life experience and enough training between teaching, a career in sales and marketing, reading and coaching studies. And I will keep learning. And I'm a good teacher! And I lead by example.

I have spent enough time around many other coaches and professionals to soak up the information and at least refer to it. I have committed enough time studying, reading, and attending courses. Enough time with life experience. My whole life has been a learning experience. Maybe I will learn more for the next edition.

Certainly, this edition feels endless with more and more strategies and overall learnings dropping in! Again, some say "*The answers are within you*" yet they don't always explain to us how to find them. I think I can do that. I know I can. Because I've walked the walk and talked the talk for six years now. I've been a sponge for this information, the secrets to life and the universe!

I think I can share the information with examples, illustrations and ease of explanation, in layman's terms that sometimes others cannot. And EMOJI came to me in a blinding flash while I was on a walk doing a live video about strategies for wellness.

Doing the inner work can start right here with this book. Next year, I plan to run a simple, easy Facebook program for you and your family or friends. If you like the book, please post a comment in my group *EMOJI: Find your Happy Face*. I will keep a list of people to notify when the program starts. I may even run a short free program between the book launch and Christmas. I want everyone to have access to everything I've learned in the last few years. I want everyone to have somewhere, and resources, to find answers and get support.

*For families: Do the inner work for yourself to become a better parent. Find strategies for the kids and teens such as those mentioned throughout the book and in Resources.

Inner healing.

I often mention *Inner Healing* in the EMOJI Model. I guess this is really like doing the inner work. To create the healing. A lot of it is about "letting go" of what doesn't serve us. Read David Hawkins "*Letting* go" or anything by Eckhardt Tolle. There are many books on healing. Another favourite is Louise Hay "*You can Heal Yourself*" which I'm currently reading again for the melanoma. It links emotions to particular organs and illnesses.

Many will explain how the word disease can be broken down into *dis* and *ease*. It has been said, our feelings and emotions can create wellness or illness. We all know about getting sick when we are stressed. Many illnesses are stress related: heart complaints, hypertension, viruses, infections and more. Even some chronic fatigue conditions can be linked to stress.

On homeopathy. I used to take my kids to a homeopath. A lovely older man called George. He taught me how emotions and feelings were part of illness. Homeopathy uses herbs and flowers and a system called *like cures like* where a substance that causes disease in some might cure others. Homeopaths look at family history, personality, lifestyle, and the disease history. Each person is unique in their treatment. There is some scepticism as there is for many other alternative health practices. I will give everything a try to see what works for me. And remember that scepticism can be fear or lack of information and proof.

There are many other alternative treatments such as Bowen Therapy, Reiki, and others which I have tried and some I haven't yet. Many have huge followings. There are new modalities coming up all the time. I think especially since I have been writing this book, I have come across something almost every week. Some are a tweak or new spin on an existing modality or technique. If you have a modality and a simple explanation, I would love to include it in my next edition. Recently, I attended an evening, organised by Beverley, with ladies at Sandgate and a lady called Vicki showed us a modality called Ortho-Bionomy, a kind of nerve and muscle testing, intuitive healing.

The Spiral. I came across *The Spiral* by Dane Thomas in Byron Bay. I was lucky to live near his mother Pat, who many refer to as the mother of Spiral. I was able to go through my own spiral journey with Pat, which was a prerequisite to *Spiral Practitioner Training,* a weeklong event. I am so grateful to have studied Spiral. It's a tricky one to explain.

Dane has incorporated some NLP (*Neuro Linguistic Programming*), a recognised coaching strategy, and some Spiral Dynamics from a school of practitioners many years ago, way back as far as the 1950s with Professor Clare W. Graves. He uses the David

Hawkins *Scale of Consciousness* I have referred to, the Chakras (a well-known energy system) and Kinesiology which is also known as muscle testing. Dane's first book was called "*Clear your Shit*" and it explains the methodology well. As I say it's all about "letting go" of what doesn't serve us.

I wasn't sure about Spiral at first, but as I learned more, I could see it was something I could add to my toolkit. It can be a very powerful technique.

I will share later what Karen said about her Spiral journey with me. (She was my first Guinea pig.) See Testimonials.

For families: Take your own journey which will in turn affect others in your family.

Inner Peace and Calm.

Finding inner peace and calm is all I ever wanted. I knew it was out there. I knew of some people who had found this. I desperately wanted to learn how. And I'm still learning. One day soon I will go to learn Yoga in Bali. I might go stay at a retreat at the Sunshine Coast where they don't speak. When I've mentioned this to people they've laughed.

Sharon not speaking. Ha ha!

And to let you know, I am learning to listen more. Just last night, I went to a women's group where we listened to a lady talk about a healing strategy called Ortho-Bionomy and there were people in the group interrupting with excitement all the way through, even though the leader had noticed the chattiness and done a short *still the mind* meditation for us to get started and listening. The presenter handled them beautifully. And I listened and thought "That used to be me."

As I drove up to my place on the river today, I listened to my young coaching mate Harry doing his *Evening Evolution*. One of the things he said while talking about unconditional love, was when someone tells you a story, to listen and comment and not be so quick to tell your story. I know I sometimes do that. Do you?

As I scroll through my phone just now, (avoidance much?) a memory comes up on my Facebook. A meme of two seagulls, where one is saying to the other: "Do you think I talk too much? I mean people say I talk too much, but I don't think I do. I may talk a lot, but tons of people talk a lot more than I do." One seagull is turned away and the one talking is in his face squawking.

I have posted one on Facebook a few times "Shoutout to those who had 'Talks too much'" on their report card. It always brings many comments.

We talk over people, we talk to fill in the gaps, we tell stories rather than listen. We try to outdo each other in conversation. We gossip, judge, justify. (See 3 J's). We argue and make jokes. What we really need is to be still with our thoughts, face our shadows and really listen. Then we can begin to find peace and calm. Then we can truly connect with others.

Peace and calm can be achieved in many ways. Some find it with mindfulness and meditation. I know I have. Some find it through improving their communication and relationships by studying things like masculine and feminine energies, or behaviour types like the DISC model mentioned in Energy.

I think the most important way to find peace and calm is by healing your pain. I've been working towards this for six years now. I've studied different styles of coaching, many of them mentioned. I've done self-mastery weekends and weeks, online studies, read the books, attended the courses, tried many modalities, therapies, strategies and have been coached by many of the best in the business in Australia and followed coaches in the United States and the United Kingdom as well as other countries. I have come so far in the past few years, and I have been interviewed by people from all over the world, have been a speaker on panels on various topics and been offered my own show with a couple of groups, one I will be starting soon and will most likely continue into next year.

I have written a chapter for a book called *Change Makers* for women with Emma. People who have come from adversity and changed their lives and now teaching others. I was asked by another coach and hypnotherapist to contribute to a book on anxiety and to focus on kids. I was also invited into a coffee table book for women called *55 Faces* with Michelle from Bali, where we wrote our story in one thousand words (challenge) and had to choose a nice photograph. Mine was taken by Frank at the beach, with Basil the Brilliant Dog. (New name thanks to Lisa, from *A Handle on Oils*. We used to call him Basil the Fawlty Dog after Basil Fawlty from the English comedy Fawlty Towers.) I'm very excited about this project as Michelle has done two books. One is for Bali women, and we will all travel to Bali for the launch in February to meet each other.

Despite all this work, inner work, and strategies, I still have had some nagging anxiety at times. I recently did Andrew's course called *Awaken* and read his book, and from that, signed for some one-on-one coaching, doing the deeper inner work. This stuff has been next level. It's helping me but also allowing me to help my own clients more.

On Forgiveness.

Forgiveness is part of the inner healing and doing the inner work. How do we achieve forgiveness? Education can help, read about forgiveness. See a coach. Try Ho'oponopono, under E for Emotions.

I learnt that true forgiveness includes total acceptance and out of acceptance wounds are healed and happiness is possible again. – Catherine Marshall.

A coaching colleague, Terri, has recently written a chapter on forgiveness which she asked me to take a look at. What perfect timing. Her chapter was titled *There Comes a Time - To Let It Go*. It was a story of something that happened in her childhood, a great illustration. I asked if I could use this quote, which I've heard before: "*I think the first step is to understand that forgiveness does not exonerate the perpetrator. Forgiveness liberates the victim. It's a gift you give yourself.*" – T.D. Jakes

I knew I had started to heal and forgive when I was asked for my bike from under the family home. I did my best to come from love. I had left the bike there for ages as I would need the trailer to collect, and the bike needed work. There were three bikes under the old family home. Craig at the bike shop serviced them for me. I gave the kid's bike to my old neighbour and the shiny and new looking serviced bikes to the happy couple with a card and ribbon around them. This was a huge step for me, and he thanked me for the generous gesture. Things between us didn't always go this well, but my recent and current work with Andrew, my coach, is changing all that.

If anyone reading this is going through separation and divorce, hear this. You will regret many of your actions, fighting with someone you loved. Get the help you need to do this well, it is possible. Contact me for ideas. I can help your whole family.

For families: Learn meditation and mindfulness and share with the family. Learn forgiveness and coming from love, not fear. Do the inner work. Teach this to the family.

Inner health.

Inner health can mean many things. To me, it's about feeling good inside. There is a probiotic in a bottle, either powder or capsules called *Inner Health*. I take this whenever I need to use antibiotics which is rare these days due to all these learnings. Mental health affects our physical and vice versa. Many say that gut health is where the chemicals for our mental health are made. I even read a statistic that said 85% of our brain chemicals are made in our gut. This is not quite the case yet it's definitely true that what we eat and drink, affects our brain chemistry, our feelings and emotions.

I have had a long history with anxiety and depression. I have learned so much about them. I have learned a lot about nutrition and have been a keen observer of how and what I eat, and drink affects my mental state. I am now working with Matty to keep improving this. Certainly, when I was drinking, my anxiety and depression were worse. Add to that a half a tub of ice cream or half a block of chocolate because the drinking would create cravings, and a lack of will power, even rebellion, as we all know, and my discipline would go out the window because I was drinking. I would start my evening with a drink and vow to not drink much and stay off the sugar. Bit by bit, it would all go out the window. I would fall asleep on the couch or stay up way past midnight, wasting time and feel like crap the next day; only to do it all over again, night after night. I was a mess. I look at photos of myself with dark circles and bags under my eyes, and I can see the fear. It was a long road to travel, to come out of it all.

For families: Join groups to learn about nutrition and gut health, learn about probiotics for your family's health. Plan healthy meals. Use fresh fruit and vege platters. Show by example.

Inner wealth.

This is one I hadn't thought of, and my coaching friend Lillian suggested this. Lillian, in her program *The Nurtured Heart*, talks about our *inner wealth*, meaning our talents and strengths. She also says *we build portfolios of greatness,* how cool is that? I love how people in my group, other coaches, and people into personal development, have contributed to the model. It's been a real collaborative effort, thanks to everyone involved. The model has evolved and developed over time in my mind, I wanted to ask the group members what they would add. I will continue to do this in the group. It's great. I only have to pose a question and the wisdom comes in. There is a real team spirit and ownership of the

EMOJI model for which I am grateful and proud. I put Lillian in touch with Tammy in Ontario who talks about our *Superpowers*. Tammy is a *Hero Intelligence* expert.

For families: See resources to find out more. Build your inner wealth and that of your family members.

Interactions. (Connection, communication.)

Someone in the group, we can't recall or find who, was it you, Karen? suggested *Interactions*. I agreed this would be a good one to include. All our interactions with others, or communication or connections are vital. When you look at any problems or challenges you are facing in your life, many that cause anxiety or depression, they are often related to our interactions with others.

How we interact is everything. I saw a video last week from Nas, one of the personal development gurus, and it was about our *fight languages*. I mentioned love languages earlier in emotions. Nas Yassin explains *fight languages*; for example, one person may want to discuss and solve the problem right away, the other might want to wait a while; have time to think about it or mull it over. This happened to me just recently with a family member.

If we can be patient and wait for them to come around, rather than push, things will go a lot better.

Interactions can be *react or respond*, mentioned in the Introduction. Think of old school letter writing where we sit and think about our response and maybe even sleep on it overnight before sending. We need to do that with emails, even messages and texts. Comments on social media. Think before we speak or act. Less confrontation. How often do we say what was said online would never be said face to face? In schools we use a strategy called *THINK*.

THINK = is it?
Truthful,
Helpful,
Inspiring,
Necessary,
Kind?

If you find yourself gossiping or bullying, judging anyone, maybe print out this as a chart?

Connection is vital. Studies show that people who have someone to talk to each day are less likely to have depression. We all need connection. Sometimes even a puppy or kitten as a mate, a goldfish. When Uncle Shane, my brother-in-law went away, he left his fish with Nonna and Nonno (Italian Grandparents) who doted on that fish. When Lisa brings her doggie Booma to see Nonno at the nursing home, he lights up.

When I lived alone in my flat then townhouse, I often said I didn't feel lonely as I had many people to talk to online. I was so lonely in my heart. I had lost everything and my interactions with my kids were full of tears and alcohol. My interactions with my ex were awful. My mum lost her husband, my second stepfather and she was grieving, as I was, and we were not interacting well. My interactions at work were not great. There were only a small handful of people on staff I could talk to. My friends were great, but many didn't know what to say or do. I did have Wilson, my home-made replica of the volleyball that Tom Hanks had in the movie Castaway. (Thanks, Sarah, for the ball and your amazing friendship over time.)

I hid so much from the world in person and on social media. It wasn't until a couple of coaches called me out, thanks Andrew and Jade, I began to let my guard down and tell my authentic story.

I once heard about a study where they gave puppies to prisoners in England, and they were less likely to reoffend because they were worried about who would look after their dog? They had a reason to get up each day. A connection. Wow! Simple.

Interactions, communication, and connection are all vital. Communication styles can come into play, just as love languages and fight languages do. Find out about your communication style with various models, personality profiles and studies in verbal and non-verbal communication. I recently watched a non-verbal communication expert explain about the Johnny Depp and Amber Heard trial. It was fascinating. I have a friend in coaching, Alan, who can predict from facial features your personality traits.

Interaction is a great addition to the model, suggested by a group member for which I am grateful.

For families: Work on family interactions. Use coaches in Resources to follow. Discuss with family how you want to interact, with respect and love. Speaking with honesty, but calmly. Consider pets?

Inspire

Last minute entry! INSPIRE! Chatting with my friend Nessy, who makes films called Inspireflix, I thought aarrgh, what about Inspire? What can you do to inspire others? I know a few people have told me I inspire them with my work. Wow! I hope this book inspires you to make some changes to your life or help someone.

Other I strategies.

Impact is part of Calvin's *WILD* program. Tony Robbins would say this serves our need for significance. The world is now full of influencers. Ideals and ideas. Interests. Independence. Introspective. This might relate to *Observe*, in the O strategies. So many strategies interconnect.

For Families: Discuss impact with kids. Look at Plastic Free boy, Arlian. Join a charity challenge. What else could you do to create an impact, locally, or in the world? A Beach or local clean-up? Create some family recycling projects. Do a RAK (Random Act of Kindness) for someone. A neighbour or family member.

Please post more ideas in the group on Facebook any time to add to the model, we love it!

Notes on I.

Chapter 11.
What's Next?

What's AFTER Emoji? Where to from here?

After Emoji, comes so much more. A wise friend and coach, Bernie, said to me on New Year's Eve: *Life is not about finding yourself but creating yourself.*

I believe both to be true now. As I mentioned back at the beginning, many coaches will say: *The answers are within you.*

Synchronicity is everywhere. Or is it just your reticular activating system?

The whole time I've been writing this book, things keep happening to fit with the book. This is caused by something called the *reticular activating system*, or RAS. It's a part of the brain responsible for the fight-flight response, conscious thoughts, and our ability to focus. It can be responsible for some subconscious thoughts. It is said, it's the part of the brain which is responsible for when you buy a red car and then you see all the red cars on the road.

While I've been writing, things just keep coming up for me. I am actively researching and asking questions in my group. I'm receiving answers every day. Today, while I was writing these concluding pieces, I wanted to write a "*Where to from here*" section and yesterday I got an invite to attend a webinar this morning. I had shown interest in a coach's webinar on *Quantum Mechanics.* This is something many people are now talking about, how we are part of the universe, maybe even "one" with the universe and how we can learn, grow, and heal to a point where we can manifest.

Anyway, I set myself up for writing, got my washing, dishes and rubbish done and grabbed a cuppa to be on the live webinar on zoom. And boy, I am sure glad I was. This was a great webinar and Chris is running a ten-week program to follow this up. This is something I'd love to do down the track yet at the moment, between my health, school, coaching for myself and coaching of others, renovations, family and friends and the book, that's enough for now. (Keep your life in balance.)

The webinar was brilliant and confirmed all I am now believing and learning. Our Aussie coaches may not be in the Tony Robbins league although many of them are top level. What they are teaching is amazing and while I hear people complaining they can't get into a counsellor or psychologist for months; I know there are many wonderful coaching programs available.

*Look around or ask about free or inexpensive programs online and try some of those, when you would normally be scrolling or watching Netflix?

Group coaching can be just as powerful or even more so as we learn from others. Or start with some group coaching then progress to some one-on-one coaching for yourself. The coaching colleges here and overseas are teaching amazing coaching models, information, and strategies to change the world and the mental health crisis. If you cannot afford a coach, then by all means wait to see your doctor to get a mental health plan then wait to see a medical health professional. At the same time, if your situation is dire or urgent there are places such as *Lifeline, Headspace, Black Dog, RUOK, Beyond Blue, Kid's Help Line,* and many more with free resources.

What Chris explained so well in the webinar is a process of awareness where some of us don't know what we don't know, which I mentioned earlier. Then along comes some learning, or even a crisis where we need to know more. We do some of the learning and growth then we find out more. We can keep learning and growing (finding answers) until we feel satisfied.

*Then it's time to create. Are you happy with your life the way it is, or can you make changes? Look at all aspects of your life and see where things could improve. Chris talked about transforming like a butterfly. Taking action to effect change. Redesign your life and being.

This was all music to my ears on a cold (for Brisbane) Thursday morning, sitting at my desk. I tried sitting out in the sun on the warm back deck and the glare on the screen was too much. I will compromise by popping out into the sunshine every half hour to hour. Basil the Brilliant Dog generally follows me so we can play ball. Or I might go to the bin, or washing line, or his favourite, way down the back to the vege patch to empty the compost. He loves this little adventure and especially when I wash out the bin and toss the water on the lawn.

Be like Basil, enjoy life!

Every little thing is exciting to him. Frank laughs at how Basil follows me around. I say yes, I am a very exciting person, sometimes I hang washing, sometimes I go down to the compost bin. Basil is not without his anxiety and insecurity like all of us. But we deal with it together. We support each other.

Eeyore, Winnie the Pooh.

It's well known that many of the characters in Winnie the Pooh were designed to describe certain character traits and even mental health issues. I read a quote that said: *"Eeyore is often depressed, yet his friends never judge, they rally around and support him."*

Dance like no one's watching, sing like no one's listening, love like you've never been hurt and live each day as if it were your last. And don't wait for the storm to pass, dance in the rain!
(Authors unknown.)

Chapter 12.
Closing Words and Thank-Yous.

I had ideas at four, as I rode my tricycle around singing Mary Poppins songs. I had ideas at twelve as I went through massive transformation and knew I was different. I had ideas at fifteen, but I was starting to follow other people's ideas. My parents had split up and many things I believed in were shattered.

I met my future husband and followed his ideas. Somewhere there, in the next forty years, although I had a wonderful life, I lost myself. I conformed to the schoolteacher, housewife then mum model. I had a short stint in sales and marketing for educational publishers and got myself into trouble with my behaviour through this. I reacted rather than responded. I stood behind the man and tried to please my mum. What I wanted to do, was jump out of a plane, skateboard, surf, don a backpack and travel through Nepal and India and climb mountains. We did do some wonderful travel for his work and some family trips for which I am truly grateful.

I wanted to go on The Voice, Australia's Got Talent, or Australian Idol. My limiting beliefs stopped that, then I would dream of it again. I don't think I have ever told anyone this secret and now here I am telling all of you. I want to sing powerful, sad, lost love types of songs. *I'm Jealous of the Rain*, by Labyrinth, that sort of thing. I always felt there was something out there, someone out there.

I used to watch *The Bourne Identity* and cry for the connection between Jason Bourne and Marie. And that ending, where they find each other again on the island. Aargh! I have always felt unrequited love was the saddest, most tragic thing, whether you lose someone or can't be with someone. I am playing *Jealous* right now and as always tears are streaming. The pain in that boy's face and voice! And the old-world music style in the middle of the song.

And as I look on my phone below the song, Denzel Washington is doing a speech to graduates at a university. He says, "Fail big!" and "Fall forward."

He tells his story from being a child in his mother's store, where an older lady prophesises that he will go far. He talks about how many auditions he went to and how he prayed and failed. And how he was eventually successful. The background music is giving me goosebumps. And Denzel's passion. He says "Ease is a greater threat than hardship. Dreams without goals are just dreams. Discipline and consistency. Don't just make a living, make a difference!"

Do listen to this speech, if you need some inspiration. Just Google Denzel's speech to graduates. If you can find the one with the music, even better!

Frank and I are currently writing a song to record, and we will take guitars and get a busking licence for our trip. Frank wrote the lyrics a while back and has been waiting for help to put it to a tune. He had some chords in mind on the guitar. I sat with him, his lyrics, and chords, and it's the fastest I have ever had a song come together! I have been writing songs since I was eleven and learned the guitar.

Now for the biggest list of thankyous ever in the whole history of time in the whole universe. Because I can. Because it's my book!

Thank you to my amazing millennial adult children, Marco, and Lisa, for unconditional love and support through the tough times, for being resilient, patient and understanding of your old Mum, who had more than her fair share of pain to heal and a new life to create. Sorry I couldn't make it work with your poor, long-suffering Dad. I had to find my own path. Thanks for being with me on the journey. And thanks to your dad for a wonderful family life, full of adventures and a beautiful home and his parents, our wonderful Nonni. And your amazing partners

Dylan and Crystal and their families for raising such amazing, well-rounded people.

Special thanks to Frank, my Handsome Buccaneer, best mate, and partner in crime who showed me how unconditional love looks. And Basil the Fawlty Dog who we renamed Basil the Brilliant, thanks to Lisa, from *A Handle on Oils*.

Thanks to Mum, turning eighty this year, just before my sixtieth, (gosh, how young she was, and I had an older sister by a year and a younger brother by twenty months) for her wisdom and patience. For my abilities in speaking well and learning. Poetry and resourcefulness. To my aunties, Robyn and Julie and Shawn too, Uncle Richard and Aunty Audrey, for being there, my cousins and extended family, especially Kylie. To all my friends and family who have supported me along the way and the coaches who have given me so much wisdom.

My Dad and Mum for the creative streak and Dad for inclusiveness. To both parents for music. My stepdads and their families for being so wonderful. My brother, Steven who is missing in action somewhere in New South Wales, we think, one day I'll find him, and my sister Kim, who passed away in her early forties, with cancer. They both had special needs and social emotional challenges and

I learned so much from them. My Aunty Jackie, Nonna and stepdads, Geoff, and Ted, all passed, for unconditional love, so vital to me.

Unconditional love is everything for healing. Judgement free, loving support is absolutely vital.

We can still have rules and boundaries. When people feel judged they feel unloved and unworthy. They are more likely to sabotage and become addicted. All for another book. Or send me a message to find out more.

Andrew, Tom, Steve, Terri, Calvin (and *The WILD team*), Harry, Paul, James and so many other coaches. Coaching groups such as *The Campfire Project,* Alan, Scott and Angela, *The Business of Smiles*, Scott and James, and the UK group that works in mental health where I was a presenter for a short time. *The Embodiment Alchemists* with Catherine, Steve, and team, Harry's group *Overcoming Cancer* and Steve's group *The I am Enough Academy*. Matty's group *The Consistency Club.*

To Karen, Simone, Neil, Kelly, Michelle, Cae, Christina, Monica, Peter, Rob, Jason and Amanda, Ann, Elizabeth, Sarah, David, and other friends who stood behind me and backed me. My Canadian mates, "The Ackos". I'm terrified of missing someone important. If I do and it's you, send me a message!

When I told people about my melanoma, I missed some really vital people. Whoops. I can think of so many more to mention. To people like Sue, Emma Karolyn, Nessy, Beverley, Gayle and so many who've reached out because of the melanoma. To my long-suffering real estate agent Kelly for looking after my home, at Beachmere. My beautiful green, inclusive and aware neighbours, Claire, Paul, Rosina and Frankie and their big shaggy dog Herbie (Disney all the way) and even their chickens, for making home great.

To my staff at my schools, especially Woody Point and Wooloowin who prayed for me and sent me a photo of the prayer table with my name on it. To all the children who brighten my teaching days. To the kids at Petrie at the high school, who danced in the rain with me when I told them the ways I have beaten anxiety and shared EMOJI with them. When a student said to me "You wouldn't understand Miss, I have anxiety." (See the story at the beginning of the book.)

Thanks to Emma for being an amazing publishing coach and mentor and Terri for being a fabulous writing buddy and friend.

I am free to be me. I am at peace. (Most of the time.)

Postscript.

As I sit here writing, my last day of writing, sending messages to people to ask if I can include this and that and say this and that, I message my kids Marco, Lisa and Crystal, Marco's wife, in our regular group chat. I haven't yet included Dylan, Lisa's partner (we have another less used chat with Frank as well) as I'm not sure he's ready for the *Shazzeffect* yet. He is new to the group; we must tread carefully. The names for the group chat have changed often, starting way back where Marco renamed it "Rough Draft" and "Good Copy". We don't recall what it was before that. We are now Supermum, Smelly Chemelly (Crystal), Favourite Child (Marco), all self-titled and Later Skater (Lisa) named by Marco when she was running late one time.

I ask my kids if they are ok with me sharing their names in the book. Marco replies "Instead of my name, I would like every instance I'm in the book to refer to me as Mr Worldwide." I reply, "You know that's going in the book, don't you?" He loves my comment then adds a GIF of a Men in Black style guy removing his black sunglasses. I reply, "Be careful what you wish for!" and he adds a smiley face. Then I add "Any other requests?" and Marco says, "Can Lisa be called Gabby Gabadool?" so I say, "Great idea, it shall be done."

Lisa added "Can Dylan be called the G fuel snorter?" Mum has to ask what that is. I'll be here all day! Lisa: "It's a caffeine powder he drinks. G fuel = gamer fuel."

Oh, my goodness, millennials are a different lot, aren't they?

Clearly the kids have a wicked sense of humour from their mother's side. Actually, that's not fair; their dad has great humour too. Then Crystal, who's humour I am not responsible for, yet clearly encourage and I shall blame her parents Dave and Jill, says "Can I be Resident Dice Goblin?" I say, "Yes of course, it shall be done." And Crystal says" hehehe."

Later, when Dylan gets home from work, Lisa says: "Dylan is fine with his name and would like to be called the G Fuel Salesman instead." So of course, I reply, "Cool, so he's selling drugs now?" and Marco says, "Use code Dilbert for a 15% code off selected flavours." I do so love all my millennials. They keep me young and "with it". Kinda, sorta.

Oh, this is fun, my book, and as Marco started saying to me at around fourteen "Do what I want." It's my party and I'll cry if I want to.

I'm grateful for humour, it's got me through a lot of tough spots. I'm so glad my kids have it. I'm grateful for my kids. Thanks guys, for helping me to be a better mum, a better person.

Now, as the rest of the book was a choose your own adventure/dip in book, so is the ending.

Thanks, dear readers, for coming on this journey with me.

Life's short, play hard!

If you're not living on the edge, you're taking up too much space! (Seen on a t-shirt)

Play hard or go home.

Or love and light, or as a good friend of mine said of my posts: "Peace, love and mung beans." (Thanks Cathy.)

The end, (or is it?)

Testimonials

Sharon is a warm, kind natured soul who is an expert in her craft. She's thoroughly knowledgeable and a great listener. She oozes compassion and is a delight to work with. I can't recommend her enough. Paul Stretton- Stephens, coach and artist. UK.

Sharon brings a wealth of experience and understanding to her life coaching. She's a gem. Kelly Southee, client, artist, and friend.

These guys are on point with their message and strategies.... Highly recommend them. 5 stars. Steve Barker, top level coach, Australia.

Sharon is generous with both her time and warmth. She went above and beyond to offer me insight and guidance, and to seek out information that may be helpful to my situation. She is honest and to the point, but at the same time easy to talk to. I really appreciate her support and encouragement. Ashleigh Wilkins, mum and entrepreneur, New Zealand.

Sharon is full of wisdom, caring and a beautiful person who works from her heart. Tegan Reid. Mum, entrepreneur, Abundance Coach.

If you've lost your mojo & need help getting it back definitely give Sharon from Tough Love Coaching a call. She breaks your life down into sections to find which sections you need help in. She's very energetic, kind & caring but tough when she/you need her to be. Sharon goes the extra mile for you with regular check-ins & messages to see how you are going. 5 stars. Bec Baker, businesswoman and client.

Sharon is absolutely amazing; I am so thankful for her help as I've gone through some of my worst moments this year. I can't recommend her enough! Rochelle Wheatley, client, and friend.

Sharon has been my dear friend for many years, as well as my neighbour, confidante, wailing wall, coffee buddy, and inspiration on many occasions. There are times I think we've been to hell and back, but she has somehow managed to make those dark days tolerable with her upbeat nature. There are so many qualities I admire about her, but the one that stands out above all other is her authenticity! No masks, no nonsense, no BS - just straight-up honest and real, and that's a quality I trust implicitly. She speaks her truth with love and compassion, and is a wonderful teacher, drawing on her own personal experience and wisdom, as well as formal education. Other reviews here have touched on many other qualities I admire, so I don't need to repeat them. Sharon genuinely cares about people and their well-being, having such a strong and sincere desire to make the world a better place. If you find yourself or a loved one in need, let her start with yours. Neil Ross. Digger mate! Roving atm.

I've known Sharon for a very long time. She's always on the level and passionate about helping others. Peter Carter, long serving friend, (See what I did there Pete?) near Canberra.

Passionate, driven and empathetic are three words that come to mind to describe Sharon. She is very down to earth and is always thinking of others. It's great to have her by your side when you are navigating the crappy roads that life takes you down from time to time. Belinda Drummond. Colleague and friend.

Sharon is the real deal. She is not some new age nutter who will talk about eating more activated almonds and drinking coconut water. Her advice I cherish. I have known Sharon for over a decade, and she is a shining star. A genuine person on whom you can rely, a person who has faced many challenges in her life and come through the other side better, stronger, and ready to share this with the world. David Cantwell, businessman and friend.

Sharon Chemello has a terrific way of connecting with people. She is friendly, compassionate, and resourceful, has a great way of understanding, a breadth of experience and great empathy skills. Thanks for helping me to find a better life Sharon. Karen xo, Karen Larkins, friend, and client.

My favourite testimonial! From Rachel, wife, life coach, Reiki Practitioner, and mum of three!

"I can't believe I have even time to review as before we met Sharon, we both said we needed a spring in our arse for the number of times we got up to our kids once settled to bed! With 3 kids 11, 7 and 3 we had noooo time. As a life coach and Reiki practitioner I thought ya my good vibes will be enough to have a knock-on effect with the kids. Ha ha you are kidding me, whilst I sort everyone else's shit out I come home and it's boom!!

My husband and I were at a point where we realised something had to change, this is how bad it got, I said No.1… I am going to end up in a mental institution or 2… We just need to be apart! Honestly this is how unbearable it got. We have so much love in abundance, but it just wasn't working. I stumbled across Sharon's page just by chance! I messaged telling her all my woes, the fighting, the anger, the not listening, you name it we had it! Jim and I spoke to Aunty Shazza on the Saturday, and she guided us so gently and realistically through what we perceived as "hard kids".

With a bit of guidance, we now see our kids for who they are! We communicate rather than shout and it has been life changing for us.

My husband and I have also found a new love for each other because we have time. I am blown away.

One simple technique Shazza recommended to get my daughter's attention has been life changing! We are now team Maslin. Thank you thank you! " (Love heart emoji.) Rachel Maslin, Reiki, coach, mum.

A Spiral evaluation. "I trusted I was in good hands from someone who had done it before me and genuinely had my back. I've become calmer, more responsive rather than reactive, and lighter for being released from the power and perspective of seeing life from my hurt, insecure and fearful inner child. Less triggered and more accepting of what is. Sharon is so resourceful and has an authentic, non-judgemental, supportive approach and style to enable participants to discover when and how we live below the line and make the shift to living above the line more often. This has had a long-lasting cleansing/clearing effect which has allowed me to move on from, understand, accept, and see my past in a different light therefore weakening its stronghold on me to live a more calm and restful life. The change is noticeable by my husband which says and means a lot.

Thankyou Sharon for being available, sharing your learnings and giving me your genuine commitment to help me make the change I needed badly." (Spiral Client Evaluation) Karen.

Appendix

List of Emoji Strategies (ideas)... *Add your own!*

Thanks, Terri, for your help with this list!

E

Exercise Energy Emotion Evolving Enthusiasm Earthing Experiences Excitement Expectations Empathy Experiment Evening Rituals Empowerment Ego Encouragement Explore Eat the green frog first (Brian Tracy after Mark Twain) EFT (Emotional Freedom Technique – Tapping)

M

Mindfulness Meditation Manifestation Music Mission Morning rituals Mastery Motivation Massage Movement Musings Magic

O

(Essential) Oils Observe Own your shizzle Own your worth Over the moon Overcome challenges Others Opportunities Outside

J

Journaling (The Three J's) – Jealousy, Judgement, Justification Journey Joy Jaunts Just be Jovial JokesJoin in Jigsaws Justice

I

Ice Man Inner Health Inner Child Inner Work Inner Peace and Calm Interaction Influence Introspective Interests Independence Ideas Ideals Impact

And many more we could add, the group is adding to the model all the time and we welcome you to do so. Facebook, Emoji: Find your happy face! Shared strategies for wellness and joy! At the time of printing. The name may change, but you will find us. Or message me on Facebook.

Morning Ritual.

Upon waking:
1) State a gratitude
2) Set an intention for the day
3) Smile
4) Breathe, five deep breaths
5) Let go of yesterday's mistakes
And I have added Calvin and Ash's
6) "What can I do to make your day better? To support you?"

Above the line:

Ownership

Accountability — Can we explore that more so I can better understand?

Responsibility

Below the line:

Blame

Excuses — Well, that's because of XYZ..

Denial

See also fixed and growth mindset, just Google.

Ho'oponopono

What are the 4 phrases of Ho'oponopono?

- Step 1: Repentance – JUST SAY: I'M SORRY. …
- Step 2: Ask Forgiveness – SAY: PLEASE FORGIVE ME. …
- Step 3: Gratitude – SAY: THANK YOU. …
- Step 4: Love – SAY: I LOVE YOU. (*Wikipedia*)

The Train Journey

"Life is like a train journey, with its stations, with changes of routes and with accidents. When we are born, we meet our parents, and we believe they will

always travel with us. However, at some station, our parents step down from the train, leaving us on this journey alone. As time goes by, other people will board the train and they will be important: siblings, friends, children, and partners. Many will step down and leave a permanent hole. Others will go unnoticed, and we won't even realise they left their seats, which is very sad when you think about it. This train ride will be full of joy, sorrow, fantasy, expectations, hellos, goodbyes, and farewells. Success means having a good relationship with all the passengers, requiring that we give our best. The mystery to everyone is: we do not know at which station we will step down. So, we must live our best way: love, forgive and give the best of who we are. This is important because when the time comes to step down and leave our seat empty, we should leave behind beautiful memories for those who will continue to travel on the train of our life. I wish you a joyful journey on the train of your life. Reap success and give lots of love. More importantly, give thanks for the journey. Thank you for being part of my journey."

Author unknown, quoted by many. Many versions.

Vision Boards.

There are ideas for vision boards everywhere on the internet. Go to my coaching page, Tough Love Coaching: Heart Centred Coaching for Families for a live video (Mellow Mondays) on how to create a vision board. Go to videos, then scroll down to "Untitled" as it was my first video for Tough Love, and I had no idea what I was doing. But it's a good explanation.

For families: Try a vision board or chart with kids, ask them what they would like to see happening for them, for the family and for the world. I have done them with my students, just by providing an A3 coloured chart or even larger, a bunch of magazines (available at charity stores, or ask around your friends and family) catalogues, travel magazines, and have a family workshop. You could do individual charts or a family chart. Sometimes one or more kids won't participate, that's ok, they have been invited. Always keep leading by example and do what you can.

Resources And References

Adventures in Wisdom, USA and international, college for coaching kids.

Yolande Alvares, speaker, author, coach, online programs for parents *Empowered Parenting*. Melbourne, online.

Rowan Atkinson, *Man Vs. Bee*. Netflix series.

Steve Barker, speaker, coach, author, *I am Enough Coaching, I am Enough Academy, Raw Leadership*. Wagga and online.

Basil, the Brilliant Dog, renamed by Lisa McDonald-Coster, *A Handle on Oils*, after we called him Basil the Fawlty Dog, after Basil Fawlty and Frankie named him Basil, after the herb.

Coach Dave, Dave Berman, author and coach, laughter coach, and *pronoia* advocate (state of mind opposite to paranoia.) *Conspiracy of Blessings*. Facebook, online.

Gregg Braeden, author, speaker. *Three universal fears*. American, online.

Russel Brand, comedian, actor, speaker, author, podcaster, *Recovery: Freedom From Our Addictions, From Addiction to Recovery,* book and documentary, British, online.

Rhonda Byrne, *The Secret*, *Magic, The Power*, and others, on Manifestation.

Breathwork, *Australian Breathwork College*, Melbourne, Facebook. Nicholas De Castella.

Dalai Lama, *The Art of Happiness*. International guru.

Dymphna Boholt, Real Estate Guru, *I Love Real Estate*. Sunshine Coast, online.

"Don't *Sweat the Small Stuff*" Richard Carlson.

Delores Cannon, (deceased), Author, international speaker on spirituaIty, and founder of Quantum Healing Hypnosis Technique. Facebook Page.

Tom Cartwright (and Nat Hodges) *DLFF (Drink Less Feel Fresh) Sober October*, addiction, and mindset coaches. Bloody legends. Port Macquarie, Sunshine Coast, and online.

Donna- Lee Clark *Happiness Life Coach*. Western Australia and online.

Bryce Courtenay, (deceased) International author of many books, Facebook run by his widow, Christine and team.

Roald Dahl, *The Minpins* and other books, British novelist (deceased), for the quote on *magic*. Thanks Magdalena.

John Demartini quote, on positive thinking, Introduction, American author, and coach.

DISC model for human behaviour. William Marston, 1928.

Education Queensland, *Good Manners Chart*, 1898.

Marie Element, *Clinical Hypnotherapist and Counsellor*. Brisbane.

EMOJI: *Find your happy face! Shared strategies for wellness and joy! Facebook group,* Sharon Chemello, with the help of many! Brisbane, Facebook, *Come join us, we have emojis.*

Evolve with Coach Ross, Facebook.

Robert Fulgrum: *All I really Needed to Know, I learned in Kindergarten.*

Corey Gaidzionis, author, speaker, coach for families. *The Little Book of BIG Emotions.* Perth, online.

Michelle Gardiner, coach, and publisher of *55 Faces*, for women, founder of *Aspire Series*. Bali, online.

Emma Hamlin, publisher, and founder of *Changemakers*, for women. Author and publishing coach. Melbourne, online.

David Hawkins, (deceased) *Scale of Consciousness, Letting Go,* author, speaker, authority on consciousness and spirituality. USA, online.

Angela Heise, coach, author, business coach, emotional expert. Brisbane and online.

Wim Hof, "*Ice man*", extreme athlete, cold therapy, motivational speaker, author, breathwork. Holland, online.

Ho'oponopono is a traditional Hawaiian practice of reconciliation and forgiveness. The Hawaiian word translates into English simply as *correction*, with the synonyms *manage* or *supervise.*

Chris Jackson, transformational coach, *Quantum Creation Mechanics*, Perth, online.

Brett Jones, *Awaken Your Ultimate Spiritual Journey*, meditation coach, speaker, author, and with Marie-Crystal Jones, *Relationship Warriors*, Perth, online.

Bernie Kelly, author, coach, mentor *A Journey with Bernie*, podcast. Brisbane, online.

Kintsugi, Japanese philosophy and craft where they take a broken item of china or ceramics and mend it with gold leaf in the cracks - a metaphor for embracing your flaws and imperfections. Quote by Kumai, Japanese philosopher.

Matty Lansdown, nutritionist, author, podcaster, coach, and speaker. *How to not get Sick and Die. Ultimate Energy Upgrade, Consistency Club. Busy Mums Collective.* Melbourne, online.

Caleb and Donna Lesa, entrepreneurs, coaches, human behaviour, and authentic sales. Various programs. Bali, online

LIFELINE (Australia) phone 13 11 14 see below for UK and USA and other places for help.

Dr Bruce Lipton, American author, speaker, developmental biologist, epigenetics, various books, studies, online.

Yvonne Lumsden, *One Love*, *Kundalini Dance and Life Force, Sacred Medicine*, tantra, cacao ceremonies, inner healing, Reiki. www.onelove.net.au

Catherine Lyall, author, speaker, facilitator, men's health, and porn addiction specialist, somatic frequency healer. *Integrated Men's Health, (Facebook) The Uncensored Threat.* (Book about men and porn) Melbourne, online.

Aime Maire, *21 days to Self-Love* course. 4 weeks *Know your Worth*, more info coming soon. Northern Territory, online.

Manish Mallas, author, speaker, meditation and mindfulness coach, *Mallas Mindfulness,* Brisbane.

James McDonald *Frequency Healing* or *Human Re-Engineering, Medi Masters.* Sydney, online.

Lisa McDonald Coster *A Handle on Oils,* Shellharbour, NSW, online.

Roy McDonald *OneLife Group*, financial, property, life coaching, personal development. Varsity Lakes, Gold Coast.

Dr David Morawetz, *Sleep Better Without Drugs*. Facebook and website. www.sleepbetter.com.au Melbourne.

Andrew Pearce, coach, mentor, stress and performance mentor, anxiety free living, *Infinite Flow, Infinite Calm, shadow work, shadow archetype analysis, Awaken,* (book coming) mows lawns! Laughing emoji face. Sneaking this in. Bali and online.

Stephanie Pinto, speaker, author, coach, online programs for parents. *Let's Raise Emotionally Intelligent Kids*. Sydney, online.

Pollyanna, Disney film, about positive thinking, bravery, and inclusivity.

Pythagoras, on music.

R.A.K, Random Acts of Kindness. Anne Herbert 1982, written on a placemat.

Reboot program for kids and schools *www.rebootingnow.com*

Lillian Reekie, and Naturopath Nate. *The Nurtured Heart Approach*, after Howard Glasser, American psychologist.

Lillian Reekie, Parenting Strategist, Parenting Support Network. Gold Coast, online.

Tony Robbins and Dean Graziosi, American coaches, running events for personal development.

Sadhguru, Indian Yoga Guru, You Tube, speaker, author.

Sue Seaby, speaker, author, coach, online programs for parents *SHE Time, Live Lighter, Shine Brighter*. Quantum Tapping, Adelaide, South Australia, online.

Chris Seto-Payne, *Ten Chi Acupuncture*, Annerley, Brisbane.

Sustainable Crusaders, Facebook and Instagram, and You Tube *Sustainable Crusaders AUS Travels*. Frank Moroney and Sharon Chemello. Travelling Australia mid-2023. Brisbane, online.

The Business of Smiles, Scott Carson, James Short and all smilers! Facebook.

The Castle, iconic Australian film.

The Campfire Project, Alan Stevens, and all around the campfire! Facebook.

The Coaching Institute, Melbourne, for coaching studies. Many other colleges and training available.

The Confidence Academy, Facebook Group for personal development, focussing on confidence. Brisbane, online. Sharon Chemello, with the help of many others, after Doug Holt, who went back to the USA.

The Happiness Co, Julian Pace and co. *Happiness Co Connect*, regular events and challenges. Perth, online.

The Inner Child Project, old content still on Facebook, Claire Huirama-Osborne.

The Kids, Teens, and Families Whisperers, Support During Challenging Times. Facebook group for families. Also, *The Teen Whisperer*. Sharon Chemello, Brisbane, online.

The Social Dilemma, Netflix, a great documentary for the whole family (older kids and teens) on the dangers and pitfalls of social media, how it manipulates us and how addictive it can be.

The Spiral, Dane Tomas, author of *Clear You Shit* and many more books, now teaching *Shamanic Sales Mastery*, *The Magick of Marketing*, *The Spiral School of Awakening*, now under new ownership, and Pat Newton, Spiral Practitioner. Brisbane, online.

Patricia Sprinkle, "*Women Who Do Too Much. How to Stop Doing it All and Start Enjoying your Life.*"

Alan Stevens, international profiling and communications specialist, *The Campfire Project, The 7 Secrets of Reading People* and more! Newcastle, Australia, online.

Eckhart Tolle, author, teacher, *The Power of Now* and many other personal development books. German, online.

Terri Tonkin, author, ghost writer, speaker, facilitator, mentor, life coach, *Connect Within*, Brisbane, online.

Tough Love Coaching: Heart Centred Coaching for Families, Sharon Chemello, Facebook, Brisbane, and online coaching. *Helping families sort their shizzle.*

Brian Tracy, *Eat That Frog*! Canadian - American author, motivational speaker. Online.

Leanne Vanderligt, *Fab, Fit Women over 50,* health and fitness coach for women.

Amanda Vodic (my introduction to Essential oils) now Channelled Astrology, *A Guide to the Soul's Solo Mission: An Introduction to the Teachings of Channelled Astrology*. Brisbane, online.

Jeremy Walker, hypnotherapist, and coach, *Inspire Hypnotherapy*, *Self Mastery and Transformation*, *Freedom From Addiction: A Hypnotherapist's Guide to Overcoming Addictions and Compulsions*. Brisbane, online. Book on Anxiety coming soon.

Lisa Wells, health coach for women, *Living the Healthy Way with Lisa Wells. Facebook.* Bridgewater, Adelaide Hills, online.

Wheel of Life, model to show areas of life we need to assess and work on.

WILD SUCCESS team. Calvin, Ash, Jason, and the team. Self-Mastery events, *The Art of Coaching, Coaching and NLP Community by WILD.* Perth, online.

Paul Williams, author, Transformation Speaker and Coach, Quantum Healing Hypnosis Technique* (QHHT*, Delores Cannon) meditation. Free E-book. Melbourne and online.

Sveti Williams, sleep scientist, author, *Sleep Academy Online. Facebook.* Brisbane, online.

Nas Yassin, *Nas Daily,* speaker, author. Israel, online.

Others to follow: *There are so many others who have helped me, or who I think might help you. Many you will find in my groups. Or just ask me, my contact details are in the front and back of the book. I have cited anyone* *mentioned in the text of the book. And one or two important extra groups.*

LIFELINE (Australia) phone 13 11 14

Beyond Blue 1300 224 636

USA The Lifeline (National Suicide Prevention Lifeline) 1800 273 8255

UK Samaritans 116 123

In Australia, *Headspace, Kids' Help Line, Beyond Blue, Reach Out, Black Dog Institute* and *RUOK?* And many other groups who help.

Books on anxiety and depression. Two great books I am reading now... *The Panic Button* by Tammy Kirkness, and *The Book of Knowing* by Gwendoline Smith aka Dr Know, both about anxiety. They are great books for teens. I bought them both at my local Aldi supermarket for $9.99. It's amazing what's out there. Help is everywhere.

Emoji Index

Where to find help for/with...

In memory of my little red bible, Introduction.

I'm not attempting a glossary here as many terms are explained within the text or you can Google. Many have several detailed definitions and are subjective, and I want to keep the book simple for you.

Also, I'm just posting the main references for the topic, for example, anxiety references are throughout the book, but will just post the best references. Again, to keep things simple.

Above and below the line thinking   66
Acupuncture   32
Addiction   69, 70
Anxiety   27-30, and Exercise 36, 41, sleep 39, cold therapy 81, and inner health, nutrition   91, 92
Baggage (emotional, or trauma) 19, 23
Breathwork   50, 80
Bryce Courtenay on dreams as part of mission or purpose   60
Bullying   67
Cancer   37, 51
Caution when choosing a coach or program   22
Conditions mentioned: PTSD, (Post traumatic stress syndrome) People with ADHD and on the autism spectrum, disabilities. 28
Calm and inner peace, see Meditation and Mindfulness.
CBD Oil   62
CBT (Cognitive Behaviour Therapy)   41

Commitment   21
Create   61, 97
Dalai Lama   52
Denzel Washington   99
Depression   27-30, 36, 92, and Eeyore 98
DISC model   38
Doubt nothing!   30
Eat that frog, Brian Tracey
Ego   46
Fears   86
Fight languages Nas Yassin   93
Flawesome, Coach Heather   72
Forgiveness   91
Frequency healing and Human Re-Engineering, James   26
For families in every chapter after each strategy
Gratitudes   75
Group coaching programs   28
Guarantee (sort of)   19
Healing, holistic, podcast with Harry   50
Healing   87
Helicopter parents   68
Hero's journey   78
High School Kids (teens) and anxiety, dancing in the rain, creating happy chemicals, an example for kids and teens   6
Homeopathy   88
Ho'oponopono, Hawaiian forgiveness prayer   72 and Appendix
Hypnosis   82
Imposter Syndrome   65, 86
Inspire   98
Journal, Journaling, see Journaling chapter, 75 and Appendix
Journey train   77
Joy   82
Kintsugi, Japanese craft, filling cracks with gold   72
Limiting beliefs   58, 79
Listening   90
Love Languages, Gary Chapman   43
Medications   28
Mission and purpose   58

Morning rituals   57 and Appendix
NLP (Neuro Linguistic Programming)   40, 58
Nurtured Heart Approach   42
Nutrition and gut health   37
Oils (Essential) 63
Overcoming Cancer with Harry   51
Parents   22
Paul, Quantum Healing Hypnosis Technique   41
Plastic Free Boy, Arlian , 62, 95
Problems   44
Puppies   94   *There must be puppies!*
Quantum Mechanics   96
3 Rs for Sustainable Relationships   43
Raising your vibration   34
React and Respond   32, 93
Reboot program   42
Repressed memories   38
Rituals, morning, and evening   34
Resourceful an unresourceful behaviours   10
Reticular activating system   96
Rules, Kindergarten, and school rules   70
Scale of consciousness, David Hawkins   86
Self-love   73
Self-sabotage   42, 45
Sleep   39
Spiral   88
Sustainable Crusaders, sustainability, and our mission   35, 54
THINK, a strategy, 94   and Appendix
Three universal fears   85
Timeline Therapy   82
Transcendental meditation   51
Trauma   41
Trauma strategy, common   14
Unconditional love   101
Unlearning   70
Vision boards   62 and Appendix
Wheel of life   58
Yoga   52

And always remember: *Dance like no one's watching, sing like no one's listening, love like you've never been hurt and live each day as if it were your last. And don't wait for the storm to pass, dance in the rain!*

By hook or by crook, I'll be last in this book! (We used to put this in autograph books back in the olden days! References to shepherds, who look after sheep.)
EMOJI: Find your happy face! You got this! Come join me, Shazza xo

LIFELINE (Australia) phone 13 11 14
Beyond Blue 1300 224 636
USA The Lifeline (National Suicide Prevention Lifeline) 1800 273 8255
UK Samaritans 116 123

In Australia, *Headspace, Kids' Help Line, Beyond Blue, Reach Out, Black Dog Institute* and *RUOK?* And many other groups who help.

About The Author

Sharon Chemello – also known as Aunty Shazza, S-Dawg, Shazza, The Families and Teens Whisperer, and Mermaid.

Sharon is 60 years young, and has lived in many locations, as her father served with the Royal Australian Air Force. She currently lives on the Northside of Brisbane, with her partner, Frank, and their crazy little dog, Basil.

Sharon has been on her own healing journey, from rock-bottom to thriving, and has rebuilt her life. A recent health scare has reinforced her belief to live life to the full. Create and thrive, rather than survive.

She is a mum to two millennials, is a teacher, a coach and a sustainable lifestyle advocate, crusader, and warrior.

EMOJI is her passion, sharing wellness strategies to reduce anxiety and depression, to find peace and calm, acceptance, and joy.

She believes we need to get out of our heads and into our hearts, to focus on love and live a happy, worry-free life.

Sharon is living proof you can transform your life. Listen, learn, become aware, raise your vibration, and pay it forward.

Wow! Who wrote this? I'm pretty cool, right? I wasn't a few years back, not at all. You can be too! Just keep stepping outside your comfort zone, where the learning and growth appear! You got this and I am here to help, just jump into EMOJI: Find your happy face! on Facebook, start there! Kids and teens welcome, safe space.

CONTACT DETAILS

Email: s.e.chemello27@gmail.com
LinkedIn: Sharon Chemello
Instagram: Sharon_Chemello_Emoji

Facebook: Sharon Chemello

Tough Love Coaching: Heart Centred Coaching for Families. Sustainable Crusaders. (With Frank) Sleep Better without Drugs. (With Dr David Morawetz.)

Groups: EMOJI: Find your Happy face! Shared strategies for wellness and joy! The Confidence Academy. The Kid, Teen and Families Whisperers, support during challenging times.

EMOJI: GET YOUR HAPPY ON!

www.ingramcontent.com/pod-product-compliance
Lightning Source LLC
Chambersburg PA
CBHW070251010526
44107CB00056B/2426